C Programming

C PROGRAMMING

Dr. Manmohan Singh, Rahul Sharma, Dr. Neeraj Kumar Rathore and Dr. Urmila S Soni

ARCLER PRESS

www.arclerpress.com

C Programming

Dr. Manmohan Singh, Rahul Sharma, Dr. Neeraj Kumar Rathore and Dr. Urmila S Soni

Arcler Press
224 Shoreacres Road
Burlington, ON L7L 2H2
Canada
www.arclerpress.com
Email: orders@arclereducation.com

ISBN: 978-1-77469-960-7 (Hardcover)

ABOUT THE AUTHORS

Dr. Manmohan Singh, working as Professor in Department of Computer Science and Engineering at IES College of Technology Bhopal India M.P. Prior to that he has more than 12+ years of teaching experience in several engineering colleges as Chameli Devi Group of Institution, Indore and Dr. A.P.J. Abdul Kalam University, he completed His academic qualifications include Master in Computers engineering, Ph.D. in Computer Science and engineering. His research includes Data Mining, AI, Data Science He is having 25 + research publications in reputed International journal, International-National conferences and 9 - patents (5 published- 4 Registered). He is publishing more than 10+book is field of computer science. He is completed one DST sponsor project.

Mr. Rahul Sharma, working as Assistant Professor in Department of Computer Science and Engineering at Parul Institute of Technology, Parul University Vadodara, Gujarat. Prior to that he has more than 6+ years of teaching experience in several engineering colleges as Chameli Devi Group of Institution, Indore and Dr. A.P.J. Abdul Kalam University, he completed B.E. (CSE) from Patel College of Science and Technology, Indore (M.P.) and M.Tech (NM&IS) from SCSIT, DAVV, Indore (M.P.). And Pursuing PhD degree in Computer Science and Engineering from Rabindranath Tagore University Bhopal (M.P.). His research includes Computer Network, Network Security, Cryptography, Data Mining and Web Programming's. He is having 13 research publications in reputed International journal, International- National conferences and 6 - patents (3 published- 3 Registered). He also has qualified GATE (CSE) in 2015. He is publishing more than 9+ books in the field of computer science and Engineering.

Dr. Neeraj Kumar Rathore is an accomplished professional holding the position of Associate Professor and serving as the Head of the Department of Computer Science at Indira Gandhi National Tribal University (IGNTU-A Central University), located in Amarkantak, Madhya Pradesh, India. He assumed his role as an Associate Professor in March 2021 and subsequently took on the responsibility of Department Head in May 2022. Prior to joining IGNTU, Dr. Neeraj accumulated extensive teaching experience of more than thirteen years at prestigious institutions such as Sri G.S. Institute of Technology & Science in Indore, Madhya Pradesh, Jaypee University of Engineering & Technology in Guna, Madhya Pradesh, and Modi Institute of Technology in Rajasthan. Additionally, he gained valuable insights from the IT Industry, having worked as a Software Engineer at Computer Sciences Corporation (CSC). Dr. Neeraj holds a Ph.D. in Computer Science, specializing in Grid Computing, which he earned in 2014 from Thapar University, Punjab. He also holds an M.E. in Computer Engineering, obtained in 2008 from the same university, and a B.E. in Computer Science and Engineering, which he achieved in 2006 from Rajasthan University, Rajasthan. His areas of expertise and research interests encompass Parallel and Distributed Computing, Grid Computing, Cloud Computing, Big Data, IoT, DBMS, and Data Structures. Dr. Neeraj has contributed significantly to the field, with a remarkable portfolio of 72 publications, including 16 SCI Papers, 7 Patents, and 7 Books in prestigious International/SCI Journals and Conferences. As an esteemed academician, Dr. Neeraj has successfully supervised seven Master's theses and two Ph.D., with several ongoing research projects under his guidance. His dedication to research and education has earned him a commendable reputation in the academic community.

Dr. Urmila S Soni, working as a Professor in the faculty of Engineering & technology, at the SAM Global University, Bhopal, MP, India. She is having more than 18years of teaching experience in various institutions and currently handling the position of Director-IQAC in the same organization. She is having more than 10 years of research experience. She completed B.E. from Electronics & Telecommunication Engineering from North Maharashtra University Jalgaon, & M.Tech specialization in Instrumentation & Control from Chhattisgarh Swami Vivekananda Technical University,(CSVTU) Bhilai , Chhattisgarh. She also awarded PhD in Electronics &Telecommunication Engineering from the CSVTU, Bhilai. Her research area focuses on Smart Grid, Micro Grid, Renewable Energy, Wireless Communication & Internet of Things. She has published more than 25 research papers in various journals of repute and conferences and having 6 design patents. She is having rich experience in accreditation and giving her services, guidance and support to various universities for NBA & NAAC preparation as an expert.

TABLE OF CONTENTS

LIST OF FIGURES

LIST OF ABBREVIATIONS

BCPL	Basic Combined Programming Language
IDEs	Integrated Development Environments
LSD	Least Significant Digit
MSD	Most Significant Digit

PREFACE

Welcome to the world of C programming! In the vast landscape of programming languages, C stands as a timeless and essential tool. Whether you are a novice programmer eager to take your first steps or an experienced developer seeking to strengthen your skills, this book is your passport to mastering the art of C programming. C has endured for decades because of its simplicity, versatility, and efficiency. It has been the foundation for building operating systems, creating applications, and even crafting embedded systems. By learning C, you are not merely acquiring a programming language; you are delving into the very heart of computing.

This book takes a practical and hands-on approach to learning C. We believe that programming is best understood through practice, so you will find numerous examples, exercises, and projects designed to reinforce your understanding and encourage your creativity. Whether your interests lie in system programming, game development, web applications, or beyond, a solid grounding in C is your gateway to success.

- **Beginners:** If you are new to programming, fret not. We begin with the basics and guide you step by step, ensuring you grasp each concept before moving on.
- **Experienced Coders:** If you are already proficient in other languages but wish to master C, you will discover advanced topics and challenges to elevate your skills.

Introduction

Major aspect of the data processing function is the logical control of programming elements necessary to ensure that data is read and processed properly and used to produce the required output. In fact, the logical control of elements within a program is the single most important aspect of programming. Various descriptive charts are used by computer professionals to indicate the logic that a program is to incorporate. We consider the following three techniques, which are the most commonly used in the EDP field to indicate program logic.

Tools used for specifying program logic:

- Program flowcharts;
- Pseudo code;
- HIPO charts.

1. **Program Flow Chart:** It is a diagram, or pictorial representation, of the logical flow of data in a particular program. The flowchart is drawn before the program is written to ensure that the instructions will be logically integrated. The concept is not unlike that used by architects, who prepare pictorial representations, called blueprints, prior to the actual design of a building. Blueprints verify and integrate elements of a building before construction. Similarly, flowcharts verify and integrate elements of a program prior to coding.

The flowchart is drawn by programmers to ensure the accuracy of their interpretation of the logic required in the program.

Notice that the coding of instructions is only part of a program; the sequence in which these instructions are written and executed represents the logic of the program. Coding errors similar to typographical errors are easily detected by the computer during program translation; errors in logic, however, are harder to find and more difficult to fix. These logic errors can often be avoided when logical tools such as program flowcharts are drawn beforehand.

The user and the programmer often work closely in refining the flowchart. Any discrepancies, misconceptions, or lack of detail will become apparent when the logic is represented in flowchart form. The flowchart, the, provides a common foundation with which computer specialists and users can bridge communications gaps. In the end, the flowchart should be approved by users and programmers before detailed coding is undertaken.

A special plastic or metal tools called a template is used to draw the symbols in a flowchart.

Most flowcharts can be effectively drawn using the template's five basic symbols. Note that these symbols conform to a data processing standard and are universally used throughout the computer industry. Thus, data processing personnel in diversified areas can understand the symbols and the logic used in any flowchart if they are familiar with these basic symbols. Each symbol is used to indicate the specified functions to be included in a particular logic diagram.

Let us consider the following problem to see what a program flowchart looks like.

Assume that we have a file each with the format shown below:

File Name	Data Type
LASNAME	char(15)
FIRSTNAME	char(12)
CODE	char(1)
TELNO	char(8)
‘‘	‘‘
‘‘	‘‘
‘‘	‘‘

The code field will contain either a "1" to denote a male of a "2" to denote a female. We would like the computer to process this file and produce a report that lists the names and telephone numbers of females only.

2. **Structured Programming:** It is one method designed to standardize and improve programs so that they are easier to evaluate, debug, and modify. The technique consists of modularizing or segmenting each program into distinct blocks.

These modules or blocks:

i. Can be written in a standardized way.
ii. Enable one program to be written and debugged by a team of programmers.
iii. Are used in discussion groups where a team of programmers evaluates the program using a "structured walk-through" of the modules.
iv. Can be used or copied in several programs.

To enable each module to function as a stand-alone entity, branches or "GO-TO" instructions must be avoided. Thus, structured programming is sometimes referred to as "GO TO-less" programming the branch or GO TO is replaced by a DO loop in FORTRAN or PL/1, or PERFORM…. UNTIL in COBOL. Another feature of structured programming is that modules are coded in decreasing order of importance. The first modules are referred to as the main module, and this is followed by subordinate segments. This technique is referred to as the "top-down" approach.

3. **Pseudocode:** As we have indicated, a program flowchart is the primary tool used to depict the logic flow in a program. The flowchart serves two main purposes.

i. Before coding begins, the flowchart assists the programmer in determining the type of logical control to be used in a program.
ii. the flowchart is a pictorial representation that may be useful to the businessperson or user who wishes to examine some facet of the logic used in the program.

But despite these advantages, program flowcharts have been the subject of considerable controversy in recent years, for the following reasons.

i. Program flowcharts are cumbersome for the programmer to write. As a result, many programmers do not write the chart until after the program has been completed, which, of course, defeats one of its main purposes.

ii. Flowcharts are no longer completely standardized tools. The newer structured programming techniques have necessitated changes in the traditional format of a flowchart.

iii. It is sometimes difficult for a businessperson or user to understand the logic depicted in a flowchart.

To compensate for some of the shortcomings of program flowcharting, a new tool has been introduced that is specifically designed to depict the logic flow of a structured program. This tool is called pseudocode.

As indicated, pseudocode has been designed specifically as method for facilitating the representation of logic in a structured program. No symbols are used, just words as with flowcharts, the pseudocode need not indicate all the processing details; abbreviations are permissible.

Using a flow-chart, it is possible, although somewhat cumbersome, to indicate a logical control sequence that is executed until a given condition exists. The following symbol is used to perform a routine until a condition met.

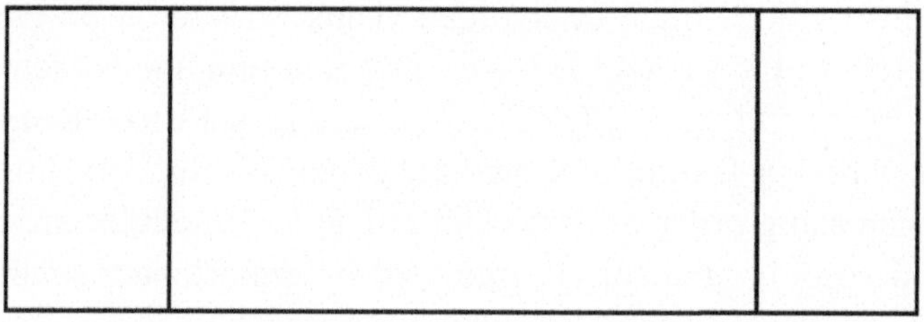

However, such a sequence is more easily specified using pseudocode.

The term "pseudocode" indicates that the technique is a code, similar to that used in a program. The term "pseudo" implies that, although this is a code similar to that used in a program, it is merely a representation of a code and not a language itself.

4. **Program Development Process:** There are numerous ways to complete the tasks in any process. Some methods are more efficient and effective than others. For example, if you want to dig a swimming pool in your backyard, you could get out your spade and start digging, or you could use heavy, mechanical equipment designed for the task. Both methods would get the job done, but the second method is more efficient and effective. The same principle applies to programming.

The program development process is a recommended series of steps to follow when developing a program. It consists of the following six steps:

- Define the problem;
- Design the algorithm;
- Code the program;
- Test and debug the program;
- Implement the program and train users; and
- Maintain and upgrade the program.

This list does not include documentation as a separate step; however, documentation is an important requirement throughout all the steps, each of which will be examined below. Although each step is presented as a separate and distinct process, they are all related; in actual practice, there may not be a clear separation between the steps. Let's address the topic common to all the steps of the program development process documentation.

5. **The Importance of Documentation:**

i. **Documentation** is the text or graphics that provides specific instructions about, or records the purpose or function of, a particular step or instruction in a program. Each step throughout the programming process should be documented. Documentation is sometimes done as an after through rather than as an ongoing integral part of the project. Approached in this manner, it can become an overwhelming burden of paperwork. If documentation guidelines are established and followed from the beginning of a project, the process will take less time and effort in the long run.

There are two good reasons to document the program development process. First, documentation leaves a clear record for someone else to understand what was done. This record is extremely important in a business environment because it is likely that the person who later corrects an error or modifies the program will not be the same person who originally designed or coded it.

Second, documenting the steps as they are developed forces a reexamination of the actions taken problems might be discovered early enough to avoid costly alterations later. Documentation is important even if you are programming just for your own use.

For documentation to be of value, it must be clear and concise, and it must be available to those who need it. Many organizations maintain a library where copies of all documentation are accessible to authorized personnel.

Several types of documentation are kept during the course of the program development process. Here are a few:

- Program specifications;
- Program description;
- Program design charts (flowcharts, pseudocode, etc.);
- Description of testing done and errors found;
- An operator's manual (user's guide);
- Maintenance documentation.

Program specifications describe what the program is intended to accomplish: they help the programmer design the program. The program description details what the completed program actually does. Program design charts outline the specific steps used in the program to produce the desired results. The types of testing done, the data used, as well as the errors found are typically recorded in separate documentation. Details on how to operate a program are presented in an operator's manual. Maintenance documentation is record of the changes made to the program and a detailed explanation of those changes.

The type of documentations kept depends on each programming department's various requirements.

Keeping in mind that each step of the program development process should be properly documented, let's take a look at each of the size steps.

CHAPTER 1

About C

Contents

C forms the basis for many advanced, highly powerful and effective programming languages. This language was the forerunner of procedure-oriented languages and still reigns supreme. A unique characteristic of C is that it is adaptable to persons who are novices in the field of programming even while intriguing the seasoned campaigners. Presumably, that may be the reason why even after 30 years of its evolution people still flock in multitudes to training institutions to gain an insight into C. One of the reasons why C is still the cynosure of all eyes is the versatility it offers. For example, the programs written are highly portable.

A program written in C can be transferred with ease from one computer to another with minor alterations or none at all. Nevertheless, C can be termed as a general-purpose structured programming language which lies at par with the best of high-level languages. So, the people who opine that C is fast becoming obsolete should spare a second thought.

C is often described as a middle level language. The programs in C are written in a style similar to that of other high-level languages such as FORTRAN, COBOL, PASCAL. The difference between them lies in that C permits intimate interaction with the internal workings of the computer. C also offers myriad operators and data types, which are designed specifically to a plethora of options to solve problems with the least possible effort.

The problems posed before you may range in diversity from bookkeeping to commercial accounting and from statistics to mathematical equations. The only way to learn C is to solve as many programs as possible with increasing levels of intensity with each program undertaken.

1.1. EVOLUTION OF C

C has survived the onslaughts of a horde of computer languages owing to its technical superiority. It was developed in AT & T 's Bell Laboratories by one of their premier systems programmers named Dennis Ritchie. The concept of C derives its origin from a primitive form of C which was called Basic Combined Programming Language (BCPL) developed by Ken Thompson of Bell Laboratories which he referred to as 'B.' By now it might not be difficult to guess that a name as cryptic as C was conferred to it because it was considered to be a modified, more adaptive successor of 'B.'

The reason why C was considered superior to B was that it offered a wide range of data types including fundamental types such as characters, integers, and floating-point numbers of several sizes. C's compactness and coherence can be attributed to the fact that it is a one-man language. This probably explains the reason for its reliability, simplicity, and ease of use. Though it has been associated with the UNIX operating system it does not adhere to any particular operating system and opens its arms for many different environments.

As the law of nature states that all marvelous things must have some aberrations, C does not deny that law and takes a setback when File Handling is encountered. Another minor limitation is that C does not have commands for input and output operations that have to be accomplished through the use of standard C functions.

Despite these flaws, C continues to be popular among the masses due to its user-friendly atmosphere and reliability. That is why programmers are infatuated with C at first sight and ultimately fall deeply in love with the language.

1.2. PROGRAMMING LANGUAGES: AN OVERVIEW

When two or more persons converse with each other there is one thing common between them. The language. Language is as important as the air you breathe or the food you eat, because it is one thing people can't do without. Similarly, since the computer is a machine and cannot understand your dialect there must be some way of interacting with it. It needs a medium of instruction and you must see the mode by which you can impart this.

There are numerous languages that can be utilized to program the computer, the most pristine being the machine language. The machine language is an assortment of methodical cryptic instructions that influence the computer's internals. In short, for the computer to perform a particular operation, a set of statements must be encoded.

The machine language is now seldom being used or you can say this is "extinct" because of a variety of factors, one of them being that it is very taxing to work with and another being that every computer has its own instruction set. Then what replaces it? The language, which is now being used to communicate with the computer, is called high level language.

Why this is preferred to the machine language is that a single statement in the high level is equivalent to a number of instructions in machine level. These types of programs are highly portable, i.e., the program run for one computer can be run on different computers with minimal or no alterations.

In the high level programs the instructions to the computer are given in the form of a program or in simpler terms a set of instructions that are to be executed. Therefore, programming can be defined as the process of performing a particular operation using a set of statements and functions.

1.3. STRUCTURE OF A C PROGRAM

After the overview of programming, it seems logical enough that you move on to the structure of a C program. A thorough comprehension of the structure of a C Program is essential in order to write a C Program.

1.3.1. A Typical C Program Has Three Broad Sections

1. **Preprocessor Directive:** Global Declaration Function Though there are 3 broad classifications, the structure cannot be strictly confined to these divisions. You embark on your program by supplying the preprocessor directives followed by declaring the variable to be used globally and then specify the code in the body of the function. If all this seems mind-boggling but as you proceed with the session's things will become clear.
2. **Preprocessor Directive:** This first line in a C program is the preprocessor directive. It connects the standard library from where predefined functions can be used. For example, to print a particular data you don't have to write a separate program for it but it will already be present in the library from where it has to be accessed. This process is accomplished with the help of a preprocessor directive.
3. **Global Declaration:** By declaring a variable, which you will use in your program to store values, the compiler is advised of the attributes of the variable such as its name, its type, and the initial value. This is done globally in the sense that it can be accessed anywhere in the program. This is entirely optional and a C program can be executed with global declaration.
4. **Function:** This is one thing, which is mandatory for a program. Every C program must have at least one function, which is the main. As mentioned earlier, the entire code of the program is given within the body of the code. Hence the program has to start with a function which is the main().

1.4. COMPILING A C PROGRAM

Coding, compiling, and executing a C program consists of different steps that will be discussed below. Before embarking on that endeavor, one must be advised that C is compatible to different operating systems like the DOS and UNIX.

Executing a program in each of these environments consists of different steps. The different steps needed for both the platforms are discussed below.

Steps involved in Turbo C:

1. **Step 1:** Opening a C program Once the system is ready and a screen opened (text editor), from the main menu you select file (ALT + F) and choose NEW. Once this is done a new screen is presented. Whenever you enter the turbo C text editor for the first time, by default a new file is opened and you can start coding your program.
2. **Step 2:** Compiling a C program Once the program is coded and is ready for execution it is compiled to check for any errors. (ALT + C) The compilation is done by a compiler, which translates the program instruction to machine language. If there are any errors in the program the compilation stops immediately.
3. **Step 3:** Error inspection This step comes into picture only if there are any errors in the coding. The errors, which may be in the syntax or semantics of the language, may vary. The line where the error lies and the type of error are displayed. Once the errors are rectified the program is once again compiled. This process continues until the program is error free.
4. **Step 4:** Running the program Once the program is declared error free you must run the program (CTRL + F9) to get a display of the result.
5. **Step 5:** Display the output The display of a program (ALT + F5) is done only when the program is compiled and executed.

1.5. COMPILER AND INTERPRETERS

Can you imagine the commotion that is caused when two people from different countries who don't know each other's dialect start talking to each other? Then how does the computer, a machine, understand, react, and execute the instructions that you dictate? Using Compilers and Interpreters

The compilers and interpreters, to keep it simple, act as translators between the user and the computer. What some people are not aware of is that the computer understands only the machine language, i.e., 0s and 1s.

The compilers or the interpreters translate the programming language to the machine language, do the necessary computation in the machine language and once the result is obtained, translate it back into the programming language.

A compiler or the interpreter is itself a program and every computer must have its own compiler or interpreter. It is just that the approaches of translating programs in both of them are different. A compiler while translating takes the whole program, translates it, and displays it back.

An interpreter on the other hand, breaks the program into sentences and translates the sentences one by one. It is preferable to develop a new program using an interpreter rather than a compiler though it is mandatory for every computer to have its own compiler or interpreter for a particular high-level language.

1.6. BUILDING LOGIC THROUGH PSEUDOCODES

As they say, a good plan is half the battle. In a similar way in C before embarking on writing the program it is essential that you plan the strategy that you intend to use.

In short, a skeletal program or framework of the code must be organized so that the entire concentration is on the logic of the program. Once the program strategy is decided, emphasis can be given to the details associated with the individual statements. This line of attack is generally referred to as top-down approach. With large programs this entire process might recur numerous times.

Top-down approach can be accomplished by evolving an informal outline containing sentences that are partly in English and partly in C. In the infant stages of the program development, the exigency for C is minimal restricting it to only major program components. Auxiliary detail is then provided in English. The resulting detail is called pseudocode.

In your example you will come across a pseudocode that is written for computing simple interest on a given Principle. The formula will be SI = p*n*r/100 and the values for p, n, and r should be requested from the user. Here 'p' stands for the principal 'n' stands for the number of years 'r' stands for the rate of interest.

Now that you have the program in bits and pieces you can put them together and design a solution. This rough solution which helps you in creating a detailed executable format is called a pseudo code. The plausible pseudo code for the above problem can be based on the following framework.

```
/* Finding out the simple interest */
main()
{
variable declaration (p, n, r)
accept values for p, n, r from the user
calculate a value for si
display the computed value of si
}
```

The above script is a rough outlay of what has to be done about the given problem. But a program cannot be formulated on this basis and thus a detailed representation of the above statements is essential. A detailed pseudo code can be scripted as shown in the next page:

```
/*finding out the simple interest*/
void main()
{
/* declare p, n, r, sum, si as floating-point variables*/
/* request a value for p and read its value*/
/*request a value for n and read its value*/
/* request a value for r and read its value*/
/* calculate sum= p*n*r */
/* calculate si= sum/100 /* display the value in si */
}
```

The a before mentioned pseudo code is a detailed description of what are the different steps involved in finding the simple interest. The above is a logic and can be implemented in various languages according to their syntax.

1.7. A SIMPLE C PROGRAM

Before embarking on writing a C program there are certain rules of the thumb that have to be followed religiously under all situations and circumstances.

Defying any one of the following laws will result in a non-executable program.

Rules To Be Followed The program starts with #include <stdio.h>. More on this is discussed later. The code for the program is written within a function called main(). Just remember that every program must begin with a main().

The entire code is written within a pair of curly braces {}.

The opening braces immediately follow the main(). The closing braces are placed at the end of the program depicting that the program has concluded.

C has a set of 32 keywords that cannot be used for any other purpose, even as a variable name.

C is case sensitive, i.e., printf() is different from printf() but generally C programs are written in lower case. All keywords have to be lowercased.

All statements in a C program are terminated with a semicolon.

These are the basic ideologies that have to be maintained while solving a C program.

Now that you are acquainted with the rules of the game you can get serious with your business and take a look at a basic C program that will help you get a feel of things.

The program that you will undertake is to display any statement of your choice on the screen.

```
/* This program prints a simple message. */
# include <stdio.h>
void main()
{
printf(“ C through your mind.\n “);
}
```

When the above program is compiled and executed, the output is displayed as follows: C Through your mind. If after gazing at the above program you are in a dazzled state of mind there is no reason for alarm because help is on the way. You will now disintegrate the above program and study each part closely, starting right from line one.

1.7.1. Comment-Statement

The comment statement helps you to identify the purpose of the program. A comment statement can be used anywhere in the program whenever the need arises for a particular statement to be explained or if some information about the statement has to be referenced later.

A comment statement opens with a slash followed by an asterix (/*) and ends with an asterix folloyoud by a slash (*/). The compiler ignores the comments and these types of comments have no effect on the program.

The # include<stdio.h> statement This is a stereotype statement that has to be present in every C program but it is not mandatory. Programs can be executed without this statement but it is considered good programming practice to affix this statement.

The main() Function The main function is the primal function that is mandatory for every C program. The whole C program is written within this main function. More on functions is dealt with later in the book.

A pair of parentheses always follow the keyword main. The braces open and close the code of a program. In between the open and close braces lie the entire compound statements. Once the closing braces are applied it denotes the end of a C program.

Output Function The formatted output function used in C is the printf(). The purpose of this function is to display the output desired by the user. To do so, the desired characters are written within the inverted quotations.

E.g., printf("Welcome in Dr. Dharm's World /n"); the above function when inserted in a C program displays the message that is within the quotations. The message within the quotations is displayed as it is and it does not affect the program even a wee bit. The"/n" makes the cursor skip to the next line Another function of the printf statement is that it can be used to ask the user to enter data for the program which will be used for computation in the program.

Say two numbers have to be added and the two values are to be requested from the user using the keyboard. Then the request for the two values is made in the following fashion:

E.g., printf("enter the value for x:");

printf("enter the value for y:");

The entered values are then accepted by the computer in a manner that will be discussed later during the session. The Statement Terminator The semicolon facilitates the termination of statements in C programming. This gives an indication to the computer that the statement has ended and anything after this should not be taken into consideration. The semicolon must be evident at the end of each compound statement.

1.8. CHARACTER SET IN C

The Character set in C has a myriad of innovative and revolutionary solutions. A character denotes any alphabet, digit or special symbol used to represent information. You are all aware of the alphabets (A to Z and a to z) and the digits (0 to 9). The special symbols are the ones on which emphasis should be laid. For your better deciphering the special symbols are listed in a table.

Don't worry about the magnanimity of the characters, because these are symbols that you come across in your day-to-day life The C Character Set Table! * + \ " < # (= | {> %) ~;} / ^ – [:, ? & _].'

1.9. KEYWORDS IN C

Key words in C are a set of predefined words whose functionality has been expressed to the compiler and whenever called upon they furnish their task with utmost comfort. Remember that the keywords cannot be used for any function other than what it is defined for, not even as variable names. If you defy this code of conduct it will result in giving a new meaning to the keyword, which is not permissible by the computer.

There are 32 keywords in C which are used at various points in a program to propel the proficiency of the language. The descriptor below is a table consisting of all the key words designed for your quick reference.

A detailed description will be given as and when the need arises. auto double int struct break else long switch case enum register type of char extern return union const float short unsigned continue for signed void default goto sizeof volatile do if static while.

1.10. HIERARCHY OF OPERATORS

All your life you have been prioritizing people or things on the basis of their power and efficiency. Well C is no alien to this tradition and plummets its operators in three distinct priority zones.

In short, if there are many operators in one equation C decides which operation is to be performed first followed by the next. For example, does the expression 4 * x – 5 * y correspond to (4x) – (5y) or 4(x – 5y)? To react to these queries, one must have a profound knowledge of the hierarchy of operations that are tabulated below. Priority

First *, /, % Second +, — Third =

1.11. DO'S AND DON'TS

To reap the benefits of programming in C one has to play the game with certain regulations barring which a red card can be slapped. That is to say, one has to play the game safely to ensure better results. Therefore, to play with C one has to keep in mind the boundaries that are set. Listed below are a few do's and don'ts of the game which will prove helpful while programming with C.

- **Do's:**
  - The main function is the first function and is mandatory for all the programs.
  - The body of a C program must be enclosed within a pair of braces.
  - All statements within the main must be terminated with a semicolon.
- **Don'ts**
  - **Forget to Initialize Variables**: In C, variables are not automatically initialized, so failing to initialize a variable before using it can lead to unpredictable behavior and bugs in your code. Always initialize your variables before using them to avoid unexpected results.
  - **Don't Ignore Compiler Warnings**: C compilers often provide warnings about potential issues in your code. Ignoring these warnings can lead to subtle bugs or even program crashes. Always pay attention to compiler warnings and address them to write robust and error-free code.

1.12. SUMMARY

Programs in C are generally written in lower case. Don'ts The keywords specified by C cannot be used as variable names or they cannot serve any other purpose other than what they are specified for.

The keywords must be written in lowercase only. The message to be displayed through the print statements cannot be given without the quotations. Initially, you were given brief details on the evolution of C.

Following this was a brief overview about the nature of programming languages and in specific the structure of a C program. Later the process of compiling a C program was dealt with after which a short discussion about compilers and interpreters followed.

Pseudocodes were mentioned and then a sample C program were disintegrated & explained and subsequently you learnt about the tabular format, the character set, keywords & the hierarchy of operations was dealt with. Consequently, at the end of the session the you were apprised of the rules of the game.

Going Over It Again:

Fill in the blanks:

1. All executable statements in a C program must be terminated with a ___________.
2. C programs are written in ____________ case.
3. Keywords in C are written in __________ case.
4. C was developed by ________________.
5. The formatted output function in C is _____________.

True or False:

1. Keywords in C are a set of predefined words.
2. C was evolved from BPCL.
3. A C program can be written without a main() function.
4. There are 35 keywords in C.
5. The comment statement has no effect on the program while execution.

One Line Answers:

1. What are the three broad sections of a typical C program?
2. What is meant by a pseudocode?
3. What is the difference between an compiler and an interpreter?

CHAPTER 2

Data Types and Operators

Contents

In the previous section or chapter, you get acquainted with the fundamentals of C. In this session you will deal with the core issues that constitute the heart of C. It is these issues on which the mighty fort of C holds firm.

2.1. BASIC DATA TYPES

The language of C, magnanimous as it is, supports several different types of data, each of which is represented in a varied manner within the memory. The data in the memory can be of integer type or of character type or of integers with decimal points. Whenever an integer or a character is used in a program, the computer should be able to identify where to store it in the memory. Just imagine the commotion caused when a character is stored in place of an integer. To avoid this, only the basic data types along with their memory requirements have been included The basic data types are depicted in a tabular format to get a better understanding of the basics of C programming.

2.1.1. Data Description Memory Range

Int whole numbers 2 bytes –32768 to %d, %i +32768 Char Characters 1 byte 0 to 255%c, %s Float Numbers 4 bytes 1.0E-37 to %f with decimals 1.0E+37 Double Numbers 8 bytes 2.2E-308 to with large decimals 2.2E+308. Now that the data types are represented in a very comprehensible pattern you can scan each data type individually. int This particular data type deals in storing only whole integer numbers and they are incapable of dealing with fractions or numbers with decimals (Figure 2.1).

Type	Bytes	Values
int	2 or 4	-32, 768 to 32, 767
unsigned int	2 or 4	0 to 65, 535
signed int	2 or 4	-32, 767 to 32, 767
short int	2	-32, 767 to 32,767
unsinged short int	2	0 to 65, 535
signed short int	2	-32, 767 to 32, 767
long int	4	-2,147,483,647 to 2,147,483,647
signed long int	4	-2,147,483,647 to 2,147,483,647
unsigned long int	4	0 to 4, 294,967,294

Figure 2.1. Data types in C programming.

The numbers which they can deal with range from –32, 768 to +32, 768. An int requires 2 bytes of memory by most computers. char The char data type holds individual characters or alphabets and they require only 1 byte of memory. Most compilers permit a range of 0 to 255 regarding the char data type. float A float data type is involved in restoring floating point numbers or to put it simply, it is used to store numbers with decimal point (e.g., 67.25).

The float desires 4 bytes for storage and has a fractional precision of 6 digits. double A double data type is also used for the restoration of floating point numbers. The difference lies in the precision and storage space. Double offers a greater precision, of about 15 digits and compilers require 8 bytes to store a double. The ranges within which the float can be represented are 2.2E-308 and 2.2E+308 respectively.

2.2. QUALIFIERS USED WITH BASIC DATA TYPES

You are aware of what the basic data types are. To simplify, qualifiers can be thought of as steroids to the basic data types, that is to say they are power boosters. The efficiency of the data types can be augmented by the use of these qualifiers, which expand the horizon of the basic data types, making it more flexible and adaptable to get into various situations with preciseness and accuracy.

The qualifiers tagged to the data types are LONG, SHORT, SIGNED, and UNSIGNED. To make any data type a qualifier, the name of the qualifier has to be tagged before the data type. long As the name suggests, the qualifier long extends the range of the data type to which it is prefixed. It can be applied to only the int and double data types and it expands the spectrum of range from a maximum of 2,147,483,647 to –2,147,483,647. A long int requires memory that is more than an ordinary int and therefore takes 4 bytes for storage.

To make an integer a long qualifier just add the word long before it. Short This qualifier is most interesting, because if an ordinary int has the same memory value as that of long, i.e., 4 bytes a short will have 2 bytes, but if an int has memory of 2 bytes a short will have the same memory, i.e., 2 bytes. Signed by using a signed data qualifier that data type can accommodate both positive and negative numbers. When a variable is signed it has the same positive and negative ranges as a regular int.

By default, an int is a signed data type. Unsigned The qualifier unsigned is tagged mostly to int and it also has the same memory requirement as that of the ordinary int, i.e., 2 bytes. So, you may ask where does the difference lie between both of them. The difference is evident in the range it offers. The range this particular qualifier boasts of is twice that of the ordinary int. To put it in numbers unsigned int has a range varying from 0 to 65,535.

Another doubt that may now disturb you is the difference between unsigned and long. One important fact to be restored in the subconscious level of the mind is that an unsigned int cannot store negative numbers unlike long. The unsigned int can be applied to other int qualifiers like unsigned short int and unsigned long int.

2.3. THE VARIABLES IN C

Consider you have some money and you want to store it in a safe place. The best place you can think of is the bank and you save it in your account, which has an id number. Thus, whenever you want to retrieve the money you can do so by flashing the id so that the bank authorities can recognize your money is in that particular account.

In a similar way you have a number and you have to store it in some safe place so that it can be retrieved and used whenever required. Here you store it in the memory (the bank) OK, so you have stored your number in the memory. But where? Why such a query arises is because the memory is so expansive and that a tiny little number can be stored anywhere. To identify where it has been stored you can name the location (the account) and that name is called variable name (account id). Whenever the need arises for the utilization of the number it can be recalled from the memory using the variable name which helps the computer to identify in which location the number is stored and extracts the number and uses it for computation. These locations can hold either an integer or a real constant or a character and they cannot hold more than one at a time. The location which is allotted for an integer can hold only an integer and nothing else. It is the same case for the other types.

Given below are valid examples:

- **Example 2.1:** The first character in the variable name must always be an alphabet. In the above example you can see that all of them start with the alphabet c. Don't include any commas or blank spaces or special symbols within a variable name. Only underscore is allowed. (Not fair is it?) Now that you have created a variable name, how does the computer understand whether the variable will contain an integer or a character or a floating point.

Well it doesn't understand anything unless you tell it folks! So now how do you tell it? To specify to the computer what type you want to store, you specify the data type (i.e., int for integer, float for numbers with decimal point and char for character.) just before the variable name.

Take a look below:

int e_sal float da char e_name

Here e_sal, da, e_name are the different variable names. Though the programmer decides the variable names it is always preferable to use meaningful variable names. For example in the above example, e_sal means employee salary, da means dearness allowance and e_name means employee name.

2.4. TYPE DECLARATION

One may tend to consider type declarations to be just another drop in the vast ocean of C's technical jargon and tend to turn a blind eye towards it but it doesn't happen to be so. You are aware that C uses variables (a, b, x, y, and so on). These variables can be assigned to any one of the data types, i.e., the variable can be assigned to store an integer number or a floating point number (a number with decimals, in case you forgot) or a character.

This assignment of a data type to the variable is called type declaration. Type declaration has to be done at the beginning of the program right after the opening braces. The process of type declaration makes programming in C very uncomplicated because once the variable is declared at the beginning, the same variable can be used any number of times in the program and each time its data type will be the same as that declared in the beginning.

- **Example 2.2:** Presume that x is a variable and it has been assigned the data type int. This means that the variable x can store only integer numbers throughout the program anywhere it is called. **int sal;** If there is more than one variable to which the same data type has to be assigned, it can be done by making it succeed the data type instead of prefixing the data type name before all the variables.

For Example:

int sno,cno,hno; float sal,id; char sname,cname; There are a few rules that have to be broadcast while exercising the task of type declaration.

2.4.1. Rules for Type Declaration

All data types are keywords and they should always be written in lower case and they cannot be used as a variable name or for any other purpose (revert to the rules).

The data types should be written as depicted above and not its full form, i.e., int cannot be written as integer.

All declarations should be performed before the first executable statement.

All declarations must end with a semicolon.

2.5. OUTPUT FUNCTION

The formatted output function used in C is the printf (). The purpose of this function is to display the output desired by the user. To do so the desired characters are written within the inverted quotations.

For example:

printf("Welcome in Dharm's World /n");

The above function when inserted in a C program displays the message that is within the quotations. The message within the quotations is displayed as it is and it does not affect the program even a wee bit.

The"/n" makes the cursor skip to the next line. Another function of the printf statement is that it can be used to ask the user to enter data for the program, which will be used for computation in the program. Say two numbers have to be added and the two values are to be requested from the user using the keyboard. Then the request for the two values is made in the following fashion.

E.g., printf(" enter the value for x: ");

printf(" enter the value for y: ");

The entered values are then accepted by the computer in a manner that will be discussed later during the session.

2.6. THE INPUT FUNCTION AND FORMAT SPECIFIERS

In your first encounter with a simple C program you stumbled upon the output function which is the printf(). Now you used to make way for the input function which is called the scanf() function. You already know that the printf can be used to request data from the user through the keyboard.

Everything's fine till now, but who is going to accept the entered characters? The scanf() does. How it does is rather an intriguing fact, which will surely keep you spellbound (if not confused). What happens is that the scanf uses something called the Format Specifiers which aids it in the input proceedings. The format specifiers are special symbols allotted to the different data types. These Format Specifiers are mentioned in the parenthesis of the scanf based on the data type assigned to the variable in the beginning. Also, in the parentheses is mentioned (Figure 2.2).

Functions	Description
scanf()	This function is used to read one or multiple inputs from the user at the console.
sscanf()	This function is used to read the characters from a string and stores them in variables.
printf()	This function is used to display one or multiple values in the output to the user at the console.
sprintf()	This function is used to read the values stored in different variables and store these values in a character array.

Figure 2.2. Basic function in C programming.

Variable name preceded by an "&" symbol. It looks something like this:

printf("enter the customer number:");

scanf("%d", &cno);

Here the %d is the format specifier for an integer.

All format specifiers must be enclosed within quotations. & is the mandatory symbol and cno is the variable name which holds an integer. As soon as the user inserts the values the scanf identifies to which data type the inserted character belongs and stores it in the memory in that location (i.e., in int or char or float). Some of the symbols for their corresponding data type are tabulated below:

%c Character %d, %I Signed decimal integers %f Decimal floating point %s String of characters %u Unsigned decimal integers %x Unsigned hexadecimal %p Displays a pointer %% Prints a % sign Operators in C Now the time is ripe to learn operators in C. In your earlier endeavors on C you noted that C encompasses a variety of operators. You will concentrated on the basic building blocks of operators and throw some light on the other operators.

Operators can briefly be defined as the tools used for solving various mathematical, conditional, relational, and logical dilemmas. The operators that you will be dealing with are arithmetic operators, unary operators relational and logical operators. Just one more thing, the items in between which the operators are placed are called operands.

2.7. ARITHMETIC OPERATORS

The Arithmetic operators can be considered the kingpin of all the operators. Arithmetic operators are tools that help us in computing various mathematical operations. There are basically five types of arithmetic operators. + Addition – Subtraction * Multiplication / Division % (modulus) finds the remainder one basic requirement of the operands is that they should be either integer quantity or floating point or even characters. You may wonder how can words be added or subtracted. This is where C proves its superiority over others. The C compiler is so ingenious that it represents even the characters as integer values and whenever an operator has to act on a set of characters it converts the characters into their integer values and performs the operation (Figure 2.3). Amazing isn't it?

Operator	Operation
+ (Addition)	z = x + y
- (Subtraction)	z = x - y
* (Multiplication)	z = x * y
/ (Division)	z = x / y
% (Modulus)	z = x % y

Figure 2.3. Arithmetic operators.

You must have been quite familiar with the above operator signs and their functions (recall elementary math's) but the operator called modulus (%) must be a bit new to some of you. Things will be clear when the modulus operator is studded in between the operands it first performs the division and displays the remainder if any, on the screen.

- **Example 2.3:** If you write as 7% 3 then the answer displayed will be 1 because 7 when divided by 3 leaves a remainder 1. The modulus operator always displays the last non-divisible remainder and for the modulus to perform effectively it is highly essential that both the operands are numbers and the second operand must be a non-zero number.

While performing the division operation if the quotient is not a perfect number and has decimal points, the division is performed after terminating the decimal points (truncation). You shall now undertake some tailor made examples that will help you understand the role of the operator s in different data types.

- **Example 2.4:** You assume that x and y are two integers whose values are 9 and 4 respectively then the application of the operator in these numbers will result in the following values.

  al x + y 13 x-y 5 x*y 36 x/y 2 x%y 1

2.8. UNARY OPERATORS

If the outlook of the name bewilders you there's no cause for panic. This is just another example that goes to prove that things that seem confounding are actually elementary. There are two basic unary operators The increment operator (denoted as ' ++ ') The decrement operator (denoted as '—') You must again be wondering what do two addition signs or two subtraction signs do. Well when the increment operator is prefixed to a variable which holds an integer it increases the value of the number by one.

Similarly the decrement operator decreases the value by one. To put is simply.

- **Example 2.5:** If you assign an integer ' a ' the value 3 then writing ++a would be equivalent to writing it as a = a + 1. Therefore, the modified value of a would be 4. Similarly, – a would mean a = a – 1 and its modified value would be 2. Another operator worth mentioning is the size of the operator. As the name suggests whenever this operator is prefixed to the operand the size of the operand in bytes is returned.

Assume that x is an integer and y is a floating point number then the size of x and y can be determined as follows:

```
#include<stdio.h>
void main()
{
int x;
float y;
printf("integer: %d", sizeof x);
printf("float: %d", sizeof y);
```

}

The output generated will be as follows:

integer: 2 float: 4

2.9. RELATIONAL AND LOGICAL OPERATORS

Relational Operators

These are few of the operators which assist you during the computation of mathematical conditions and they will frequently spring up in due course of this book. When used between two operands they establish a relation between them, saying whether the first operand is less than the other one or greater than or equal to the other. Just like arithmetic operators these are also elementary signs that you have been coming across from your school years. There are four types of relational operators in C that are familiar. ca

< Less than <= Less than or equal to > Greater than >= Greater than or equal to Apart from the relational operators there are a couple of equality operators which are noteworthy: Oper

== equal to!= not equal to Logical Operators Now that you are thorough with relational operators you can take a peek into the logical operators which are of two types on to AND, the OR. Ope

&& And || Or! Not Before concluding about on the operators a few points to note about the logical operators is that an 'and' operator becomes true if and only if both the operands satisfy the condition and the 'or ' operators become true if at least one of the operand satisfies the condition.

A assume that a certain program has to perform certain steps based on the condition that x < 15 and y == 8. To concatenate these two statements using the "and " operator it is coded in the following manner (x < 15 && y == 8). Similarly, the " or "operator can be used to check if any one of the following is true as in (Figure 2.4):

(x < 15) || (y == 8)

Operators	Operations
==	Equal to
!=	Not Equal to
>	Greater than
>=	Greater than equal to

<	Less than
<=	Less than equal to

Figure 2.4. Relational and logical operators.

2.10. CONSTANTS IN C

One common thing that you might have noticed in your earlier endeavors to understand C is that the procedures being explained help you gain a fairly good idea on the subject. The particular concept which you are about to learn right now just helps you to create short cuts so that programming C will be as simple as tying your shoe laces. Constants are created in C so that they can be used any number of times in the program. For example, If in your computations the symbol pi is to be used, then you have to declare pi as a real constant and assign it a value 3.14285714. So, whenever in the program, computation has to be done with pi instead of using the complete number you just address it as pi (e.g., 24 * pi + 35 * pi) C constants can be divided int two broad categories Primary constants Secondary constants.

The further delineation of C constants is depicted below: C Constants Primary Constant Integer Constan Real constant Character Const Secondary Constants Array Pointer Structure Union Enum, etc. At this juncture the discussion is limited to only primary constants viz. Integer, real and character constants. For the establishment of these types of constants certain guidelines have been laid down which have to be put into practice.

2.11. A PROGRAM IN C

Now that you have learnt the tricks of the trade it's time to put them in practical application. In short it's show time folks! You will now write a C program which will use most of the skills which you have acquired. The program below will be studded with variables, data types, input /output functions and some other details which will have an explanation once the program is completed. For your convenience the lines are numbered but these numbers do not appear in a C program. Loaded with technical jargon you will now amplify your knowledge by venturing into your first ever C program. Before you actually take your first shot spend a few moments to recapitulate the aforementioned 12 pointers.

This is essential because all that you thought was unexciting and dreary will actually play a pivotal role in carving your program. You are presented with a very undemanding little program that will help you grasp the basic functioning of a C program.

```
/*Example to accept values & display back to screen*/
#include<stdio.h>
void main()
{
int a,b;
printf("Enter the value of a:");
scanf("%d",&a);
}
```

2.12. CONSTANTS IN C

One common thing that you might have noticed in your earlier endeavors to understand C is that the procedures being explained help you gain a fairly good idea on the subject. The particular concept which you are about to learn right now just helps you to create short cuts so that programming C will be as simple as tying your shoe laces. Constants are created in C so that they can be used any number of times in the program. For example, if in your computations the symbol pi is to be used, then you have to declare pi as a real constant and assign it a value 3.14285714.

So whenever in the program, computation has to be done with pi instead of using the complete number you just address it as pi (e.g., 24 * pi + 35 * pi) C constants can be divided int two broad categories Primary constants Secondary constants The further delineation of C constants is depicted below:

C Constants Primary Constant Integer Constan Real constant Character Const Secondary Constants Array Pointer Structure Union Enum, etc. At this juncture the discussion is limited to only primary constants viz. Integer, real and character constants. For the establishment of these types of constants certain guidelines have been laid down which have to be put into practice.

2.13. A PROGRAM IN C

Now that you have learnt the tricks of the trade it's time to put them in practical application. In short it's show time folks! You will now write a C program which will use most of the skills which you have acquired. The program below will be studded with variables, data types, input /output functions and some other details which will have an explanation once the program is completed. For your convenience the lines are numbered but these numbers do not appear in a C program. Loaded with technical jargon you will now amplify your knowledge by venturing into your first ever C program. Before you actually take your first shot spend a few moments to recapitulate the aforementioned 12 pointers. This is essential because all that you thought was unexciting and dreary will actually play a pivotal role in carving your program. You are presented with a very undemanding little program that will help you grasp the basic functioning of a C program.

```
/*Example to accept values & display back to screen*/
#include<stdio.h>
void main()
{
int a,b;
printf("Enter the value of a:");
scanf("%d", &a);
}
```

2.14. DO'S AND DON'TS

while constructing variable names.

The maximum length of a variable name is 8 characters (and you better stick to 8), and it can be a combination of alphabets, digits, and underscores only (nothing else).

- **Do's**
  - **Choose the Right Data Type**: Select the appropriate data type for your variables to conserve memory and ensure your program runs efficiently. For example, use int for whole numbers and float or double for floating-point numbers.
  - **Use Parentheses for Clarity**: When writing complex expressions, use parentheses to clarify the order of operations. This can help prevent errors and make your code more readable.
- **Don'ts**
  - **Avoid Unnecessary Data Type Conversions**: Minimize unnecessary conversions between data types, as these can

lead to loss of precision or unexpected results.

- **Avoid Division by Zero:** Always check for and avoid division by zero, as it can lead to runtime errors and crashes.
- **Don't Mix Data Types Without Care:** Mixing data types in expressions can lead to unexpected results. Ensure compatibility and use explicit type casting when necessary.

Going Over It Again:

Fill in the blanks:

1. The data type for storing a integer and a character respectively are ________and ________.
2. The unsigned int has a range varying from ________ to ____________.
3. The maximum length of a variable name is __________ characters.
4. The ________ makes the cursor skip to the next line in an output statement.
5. For incrementing the variable the __________ sign is used.

State True or False:

1. All declaration should be made before the first executable statement.
2. The declarations are terminated with a colon.
3. The first character in the variable name need not necessarily be an alphabet.
4. The variable name can be compiled of only alphabets, integers, and underscores.
5. The format specifier for an integer type is %d.

One Line Answers:

1. What are the different types of operators in C?
2. What are the four basic data types in C?.
3. What are the different types of relational operators?

CHAPTER 3

Control Statements

Contents

After familiarizing ourselves with the basics and the do's and don'ts of C programming I guess it's time for us to march forward and excavate areas that makes C as dominant as it is. The last two sessions you can say was just the trailer and the remaining part of the iceberg begins from here. Then one may ask what's the fun in learning so much in the first session and when do we put it into practice. You put it into practice right from now. This session deals with the situations where C uses it's paraphernalia to control the functioning of a program or to say it directs its statements how to act in particular situation.

3.1. WHY CONTROL STATEMENTS?

Well that's an interesting query. One may ask that when C is such an omnipotent language with so many features and disciplines where does the need arise for incorporating separate control statements. Well that's a tough one, but as mentioned in the earlier session with so many different functions being carried out by C it needs some kind of a managerial system which instructs the computer what function has to be performed at which time. The control statements act as a manager. You will be amazed at the amount of functions the different control statements handle.

For example in a program you may have a statement in which a multiplication operation is to be performed and in the next an addition operation and after the next line there may be a statement which may want itself to be repeated 8 times and another statement may like itself to be skipped and attended to at a later stage.

All these conditions are managed by the control statements. You have had a glimpse of the different types of control statements in the previous session and now is the time to get into the thick of the things. You have seen the broad classification of the control statements in the earlier session, here is the various subdivisions that they possess represented diagrammatically.

Control Statement Sequence Decision Loop Case if ifelse while dowhile switch goto for The sequence control structure is one of the basic uncomplicated control statements. The idea is very simple. In the sequence control instructions the statements to be executed are done so in a serial manner one after the other.

The C compiler first executes the opening line and then moves on to the next and so on in a serial fashion and the entire program is executed in this manner. For example if the first statement requires the computer to perform a mathematical operation then when the compiler comes across this statement it computes the operation and stores the answer in the memory and only then advances to the next line. Decisions! Decisions! Decisions! It is one of the difficult jobs to do at any place at any time. The reason why this is the most difficult activity in our life is because before taking a decision, whether right or wrong the pro's and con's must be weighed and then a decision can be taken.

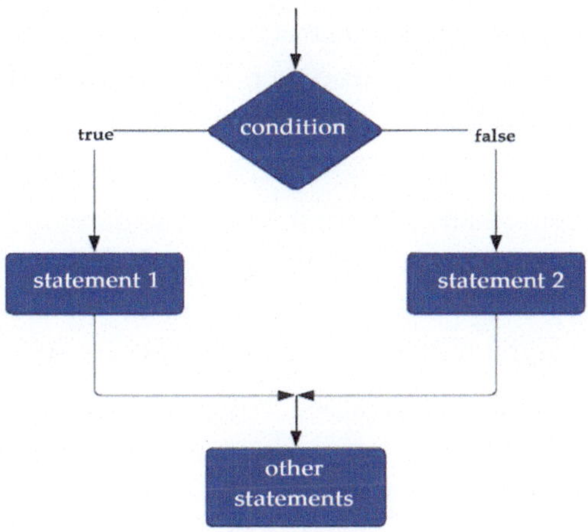

Figure 3.1. Flow diagram control statements.

There is no instant formula or readymade decisions that can be employed upon encountering a particular decision. But C has. C uses these options to counteract a particular situation. The result can be obtained on fulfilling the conditions.A decision control instruction can be employed in C using the following statements The if statement The if else statement The conditional operators Now let us understand the concepts behind each statements (Figure 3.1).

3.2. THE IF STATEMENT

The if statement reacts on a particular condition that follows the if. Unless the condition after the if is satisfied the statements following it will not be executed. It is like a person says " if I am paid Rs.100 then the work will be done by me."

In the above example it is noticed that if the person is paid Rs. 100 (i.e., the condition becomes true) only then the work will be done by him otherwise the work will not be done by him (condition becomes false). Here the condition is the payment of Rs. 100 and the statement to be executed if the condition is true is, the work being done. Since the computer cannot decipher if we write it in normal English we have to write it in a from which is understandable by the computer. The general format is specified as below:

if (this condition is true)

execute this statement; now one may ask why only the word if why not any other word. Well what the keyword if does is that it intimates the compiler that a decision control instruction follows it and if the condition in the parentheses turns out to be true then the following statements are to be executed but if the condition is not satisfied then none of the statements are to be executed.

The conditions are to be specified within the parentheses. Why? because once a statement is written the parentheses and it follows the if the compiler recognizes that it is a condition and its truth or falsity is to be checked. This is done by means of the relational operators of C (<, >, <=, >=, ==, !=).

Using these relational operators it is possible for us to compare two values whether they are equal or one is greater than the other or one is less than the other and so on. x== y x is equal to y x! = y x is not equal to y x < y x is less than y x > y x is greater than y x <= y x is less than or equal to y x >=y x is greater than or equal to y Multiple Statements using if The above example that was explained was good for only one statement after if.

But if we want to execute multiple statements after if can we do it? taking the above example we can explain saying that the person says " if I am paid Rs. 100 the work will be done by me and I will work regularly and I will finish the work within 5 days." Here three actions are being performed only with one condition sequentially, i.e., the first action is work is being done, the second action is the person will come regularly and the third is the work will be finished within 5 days.

Now comes the problem of writing in C. the format is similar to that explained above with minor additions which are the statements have to be written one below the other and all the statements should be enclosed within a pair of curly braces. The general format looks something this:

if (this condition is true)

{

execute this statement;

execute this statement;

```
execute this statement;
}
```

3.3. THE IF-ELSE STATEMENT

Playing with the if statements we discovered that the if structure executed a statement or a group of statements only if the condition was true but did nothing if it was false. Did anyone want to make something happen when the condition became false instead of let it go waste. Dennis Ritchie did. Well what happens in if else is that even if the condition turns false a statement is executed.

That is to say a statement is executed if the condition is true but if the condition is not fulfilled even then a statement is executed. Lets consider the dialogue if it rains I will wear a raincoat otherwise I will wear a sweater. It must have been quite clear by now that either way an action is performed. Let's put it the way it is actually written in C and understood by it.

```
if (this condition is true) execute this statement;
else execute this statement;
```

Even in this type of control structure the condition is specified within the brackets and the statements are terminated with a semicolon(;). /*program to find the greater of the two numbers*/ 2.#include<stdio.h>

```
void main()
{
int a,b;
printf("enter the value of a:");
scanf("%d", &a);
printf("enter the value of b:");
scanf("%d", &b);
if(a>b)
printf("a is greater than b");
else
printf("b is greater than a");
}
```

In line 5 the initializing of the variables is done Line 6 and 8 request the user to enter the values for a & b Line 7 and 8 accept the values entered by the users and stores it in the according to its data type Line 10 is the condition checking statements were the given conditions is evaluated. Here the two numbers are compared and checked to see which one is greater. If the value of a is greater than b then the output function in line 11 is executed and displayed.

Similarly if the value of b is greater than a then the output function in line 13 is executed and displayed. Nested if else Before we move on to the next concept there is a small feature of the if structure which helps us with effective programming of the decision control structure. To put it simple it is using an if else within an if else. It is like you have two concentric circles and one circle is enclosed within the outer circle.

While compiling the outer if condition is checked for validity if it true then that statement is executed but if it turns to be false then the inner if else condition is checked. That is instead of a statement an if else is included. If it is true then that statement is executed but if false the last else statement is executed. The nested if else are formatted in the following way. Before we actually venture into sophisticating ourselves with the different loop statements let us fathom the broader aspect of looping. Looping can be depicted as a cycle of events taking place incessantly.

For example, the workers say that the strike will continue until our demands are met. The above implies that a process will continue until a condition is met. Once the condition is met the cycle terminates. But it is not as literal as it seems in C programming. To perform a particular iteration a set of statements have to be dispatched but fortunately in C these statements delimit themselves to only a modest amount of statements when compared to other languages.

There are three ways by which the loop statements can be coded and they can be done effectively For, While, Do while.

3.4. THE FOR STATEMENT

The for brought about a mutiny in the world of C programming. Programmers who had a whiff of the for turned a blind eye towards the rest of the breed. They found so much solace in the for that they found the rest only worthy of warming the shelves. But what is that makes the for so popular among the masses? A single loop statement. The specialty of the for is that the entire loop structure which used to last for three lines in the earlier endeavors was condensed to only one solitary statement. Stupendous isn't it? this is how for seduces many programmers who are steady with any of the above control structures. The one for statement performs three functions which earlier had to be written in three separate statements. They are Initializing Condition Incrementing The general format of the for statement is:

for(initialize;condition;increment)

execute this statement;

Initialize: this expression initializes the particular variable to a set value, e.g., x = 0; or x = 1; Condition: this expression seta the condition for the statement to be executed.

e.g., x < 9; or x <=9; Increment: this expression increments the loop each time until the condition is met.

- **Example 3.1:**

x++ Between each of these expressions there must exist a semicolon.

```
/*program to display numbers from 0 to 10 */ 2.#include<stdio.h>
void main()
{
int i;
for(i=0;i<=10;i++)
{
printf("%d", i);
}
}
```

The above is a simple program to display numbers from 0 to 10. Line number 5 sees the declaration of the variable I which is of type int Line numbers 6 is the one we have to concentrate on. Because the for statement starts here. As you can see the variable I is initialized to 0, the condition for I is mentioned and the incrementing of I is all done in a single for statement. When this statement is written I is initialized to 0, the conditions is set that it must be less than or equal to 10 and I should be incremented each time the statements below are executed. Line number 8 is the output statement which is executed each time the condition is satisfied.

3.5. THE WHILE LOOP

Now that we have a lucid sketch of what looping is, we can probe into the intricacies of the different looping concepts by ripping them one by one starting with while Comparing with the if statements we can declare that only if the condition is true the desired statements will be executed else some other but in while until a particular condition becomes true the desired statements will be executed. Just recall the afore-mentioned example until our conditions are met the strike will continue. This concept will be cloudless with the following example:

```
#include<stdio.h>
void main()
{
int i=1
while (i<=20)
{
printf(“%d”, i);
i++;
}
}
```

Since you are aware of the first few lines our area of concern will be the loop structure. The first loop statement, i.e., line number 4 is the initializing statement, i.e., it is setting the variable to a particular value from where the looping has to begin. Count is the variable and its initial value is 0. Line number 5 is where the loop starts. The while statement and the condition is also mentioned here. The condition here stated is that until the value of count becomes 10 execute the below statement. Line number 7 is the executable statement, i.e., until the condition is satisfied the statement is to be executed. The last statement, i.e., line number 8 is a new and important statement. Using this we increment the loop we make the compiler to execute the loop structure one more time. Whenever the compiler encounters this statement it is reminded that it has to go over the loop once more. This is done until the condition is satisfied.

3.6. THE DO WHILE STATEMENTS

In the do while the statements to be executed are coded before the condition is fulfilled. That is to say the particular loop is executed only if the condition following it is satisfied. In format it can be put as follows:

```
do this statement;
```

```
while (this condition is true)
```

There can be multiple statements between the do and the while. The above example can be dealt with here:

```
/*program to display numbers from 0 to 10*/ 2.#include<stdio.h>
void main()
{
int i=0;
do
{
printf("%d", i++);
}
while(i<=10);
}
```

Here the only difference apart from switching the statements is that the incrementing of the variable is done within the printf. Since we are already aware of the first few statements we will proceed to line number 5 where like in the earlier example the initializing is done. Here the variable I is initialized to value of 0. Coming to line number 6 do statements is given here followed by the statements to be executed. The do statement open with a brace. The executable statement is the one in line number 8 which is the printf statement. The important thing to note is that the increment statement is included within the printf statement. This is followed by the conditional statement which is line number 10. Where the conditions is checked here the conditions is that the values of I should be less than or equal to 10. Until this conditions is satisfied the compiler required to do this statement above the conditions.

3.7. THE BREAK STATEMENTS

The break is an effective statement in C programming in the way that it can be used to exit from the loop without fulfilling the condition. That is to say that the break barks to the control that once this statement is encountered it should stop the process of looping and hop to the first statement that is present after the loop. In this the loop is processed at least once that means that the condition is evaluated and the statements are executed at least once.

```
#include<stdio.h>
```

```
void main()
{
int i;
for(i=0;i<=10;i++);
{
if(i==5)
break;
printf("Hi Honey");
}
}
```

Line number 4 is the declaration of the variable i. Line number 5 is the loop statement in which we use for statement in which variable i is initialized to 0, the conditions set that its value should not exceed 10 and i should be incremented each time the statements are executed. Line number 7 is where the variation lies whenever the if condition is satisfied the loop is supposed to break or discontinue. So, in the above program the output will be such that until i reaches 5 the printf statement is executed but once i reaches 5, i.e., the if conditions is satisfied the loop is to be terminated thus the output will be like this:

Hi Honey Hi Honey Hi Honey Hi Honey Hi Honey

3.8. THE CONTINUE STATEMENTS

Sometimes the need may arise that a particular set of statements be ignored and the loop be recalled. This can be done by using the continue statement. What happens is that wherever the continue statement is placed, the control ignores the rest of the statements and reverts back to the beginning of the loop inevitably. The continue statement can be incorporated within a while, do while, or a for statement.

It is written simply as:

```
continue;
#include<stdio.h>
main()
{
int i;
for(i=0;i<=10;i++)
```

```
{
if(i==5)
continue;
Printf("hello");
}
}
```

This program is quite similar to the above program with slight variations In this program when the if conditions is satisfied, i.e., i is equal to 5 the loop will be recalled immediately without executing the printf statement. But when i turns out to be 6 the output statement is printed until the rest of the for condition is satisfied.

That is to say the printf statement will not be executed only once during loop when the value of i will be equal to 5. The Case Control Structure Very often in our life we come across circumstances where we have to make one choice from a medley of options.

Like you embark on writing a competitive exam and you discover that you have to make a choice from an option of five choices or you have to go to a movie and you have to decide which to gawk at from a battery of options that are being aired. C is no alien to this attitude. To accommodate these types of situations Ritchie developed.

3.9. THE SWITCH STATEMENT

Using the switch statement an array of options are displayed from which the user has to make a choice and based on the selection the corresponding answer is displayed. What happens internally will be conversed in a few moments from now. The keywords used in this kind of control structures are switch, case, break, and default. The general format of the switch statement is as follows:

```
switch(choice)
{
case expression:
statement;
statement;
break;
case expression:
```

```
statement;
statement;
break;
case expression:
statement;
break;
default:
statement;
}
```

Lets disintegrate the above format and study the different parts. The first statement is the switch statement followed by a pair of parentheses in which the word “choice” is given. This accepts the choice that the user makes. The case can be baptized only with either integers or characters nothing else (not even floating point).

- **Example 3.2:**

```
case1
case2
case3 or
case a
case b
case c
```

Based on the choice that the user makes the executable statement in that particular case is activated. The next thing to be discussed is the “case.” within each of these is the options to be performed specified. each case has a particular set of statements to be executed. Whenever a particular case is selected the statements in the case are executed.

The break has already been discussed but the efficiency of the break can be best noticed in the switch statements. you have noticed that the break statements are used at the end of each case. This is done because it notifies the control that once the case has been executed the control should not proceed any further.

The default takes charge when the option entered by the user does not match with the given case. When no match is found with any of the given case the statements in the default are executed.

- **Example 3.3:**

```
#include<stdio.h>
void main()
{
char c;
printf("Enter the alphabet: ");
scanf("%c", &c);
switch (c)
{
case 'a':
printf("A is a vowel");
case 'e':
printf("E is a vowel");
case 'i':
printf("I is a vowel");
case 'o':
printf("O is a vowel");
case 'u':
printf("U is a vowel");
default:
printf("Is a consonent");
}
}
```

3.10. THE GOTO STATEMENT

As the name suggests the goto statements revise the normal progression of the program execution by reassigning the control to some other part of the program. Alongside the goto is written an identifier (any character name), which bellows to the control that it should park itself, wherever the identifier is present later in the program. You should write the same identifier name the place where the control is desired to jump.

Once the control jumps to the identifier it executes the statements below the identifier. The identifier is otherwise called the label. It should be followed by a colon (:). However, useful the goto statement may seem the goto is generally not preferred in programming because it can wreck a programmers life.

The general format is as below goto identifier name; The identifier may be placed any where in the program after the goto statements in the following way identifier name: executable statements;

```
/* program using the goto*/
#include<stdio.h>
main()
{
int i;
printf("enter the number");
scanf("%d", &i);
if(i==5)
goto rep;
printf("hello");
rep:
printf("bye");
}
```

In this program once value for I is entered by the user and accepted by the computer the condition which is line number 8 is checked. If the condition, i.e., the value is equal to 5 becomes true the go to statement in line number 9 is executed and the control is passed on to REP which is in line number 11 and the statement s there by are executed, i.e., the word bye will be displayed. If the condition is not satisfied the control ignores the go to statement and executes the statement in line number 10 and 12, i.e., both Hello and Bye are displayed.

3.11. TERNARY OPERATORS

After roughing out the session in detail there is one minor detail which has to be taken care. This is called the ternary operators or it is other wise called the conditional operators. This can in other words be called the if else statement with style. It is a very neatly modified if else one can put it.

The general format is as follows:

(condition)? expression1: expression2

The above syntax states that if the condition in the brackets is evaluated to be true then expression 1 is to be returned but if it turns out to be false then expression 2 has to be returned. In short the question mark(?) resembles the if statement and the colon(:) the else statement.

Things will be unambiguous when the following example is comprehended.

```
#include<stdio.h>
main()
{
int a, b;
printf("enter a value for a:");
scanf("%d", &a); b=(a>6? 2: 3);
printf("the value of b is:%d",b);
}
```

In the above example one can observe that the condition to be validated is whether the entered number for a is greater than 6 or not. If the number is greater then the number 2 must be stored in b, if it not greater then the number 3 is to be stored.

3.12. DO'S AND DON'TS

- **Do's:** The *if* statement is executed only if the condition following it becomes true. The condition should be enclosed within a pair of parenthesis. The statements following the condition should be terminated using a semicolon. In the for statements the initialization, condition, and the incrementation is done within a pair of parenthesis. Between each of the expressions in the for loop there must be a semicolon. The label in a goto should be followed by a colon.
- **Don'ts**: The choice within the parenthesis of the switch case cannot take a floating point. The goto should be avoid as far as possible.

3.13. SUMMARY

After having your stint with the brass tacks of C in the previous session you sharpened your skills by deciphering the control statements in this session. The session took off with the decision control statements which was the if statements followed by a variation of the if called the ifelse. Then you entered the loop structure and the while, do while and the for statements were learnt. The case control structure was then discussed which dealt with the switch case. The rest of the gang which involved the break, continue, exit, and the goto was later discussed and the session was concluded with the conditional operators.

Going Over It Again:

Fill in the blanks:

1. The two types of decision control structure are _________ and _________.
2. For the loop to be recalled the _________ statement must be used.
3. Between the expression in a for loop a ___________ is a must. 4. The loop structure in which the initializing, incrementing, and the condition is also set in a single statement is the _________ loop.

State True or False:

1. Ternary operators are otherwise known as Conditional operators.
2. Using of goto statements is generally encouraged.
3. Break statement is used to exit from the loop.
4. The process of loop will continue until the condition is met. 5. A default statement is a must for a switch case.

One Line Answers:

1. What are the different types of loop controls?
2. What art the keywords for switch case?
3. What is the need of break statement in switch case?
4. What is the advantage of for loop over while loop?

CHAPTER 4

Arrays

Contents

4.1. AN INTRODUCTION TO ARRAYS

In the previous sessions you have come across various methods of storing a particular number or character in the memory using variables. To accomplish this feat, a variable was needed and if 4 numbers were used, 4 variables were used. Now if you have to store 10 numbers? Quite possible one might say, but if 134 numbers have to be stored and retrieved whenever obligatory, is it still possible?

With arrays, it is. You may ask why didn't you start with arrays in the first place? You needed to have some fundamental understanding of data types and their behavior in order to learn arrays. Moreover the concept of arrays depends on other data types, which was meant to facilitate the storage of copious amount of numbers in a single variable. One cannot imagine creating an array for a single number and wasting an entire consignment of space in the memory. It would be like buying a dozen books and ultimately using only one and dumping the rest in the garbage.

Thus arrays can be defined as a collection of similar elements. In your context an array of elements can be formed only if all the elements are of one particular data type, i.e., all of them are either integer or character or a floating point number, but there cannot exist an array which hosts an amalgamation of these data types.

4.2. ADVANTAGES OF ARRAYS

The usage of arrays is crucial to any professional programming. Arrays just make the life of a programmer a bit easier. Prima facie, it relieves him of the burden of having to keep naming the variables. They simply follow the good old slotted rack principle. An array is a single variable holding multiple data. Each data is referred to by its slot number. If for instance, you wish to store a list of items, you could just name the variable 'item,' and keep storing the data by referring to item(1), item(2), item(3), etc. It may sound pretty simple but the magnitude of work that can be accomplished using arrays is praiseworthy.

To gain a better insight into the advantages of arrays consider a simple example:

```
main()
{
int a; a=2; a=4;
```

```
printf("a=%d", a);
}
```

The value that will be displayed will obviously be 4 because once another value is assigned to an existing variable with a value, the previous value is lost. The inference to be drawn is that without arrays a variable cannot store more than one value. After the elements are arranged in an array any element in any position can be retrieved without any hassles. Using arrays sentences in English can be stored in the memory using what you call character arrays, which are otherwise called strings.

4.3. TYPES OF ARRAYS

Before you get down to the brass tacks of using arrays it wouldn't harm you in any way if you had a shade more insight about the taxonomy of the arrays, into how many types they are classified and their functionalities. To begin with, the arrays are dichotomized broadly into two distinctive types. Single dimensional Arrays Multidimensional Arrays The intricacies of the above off springs of the arrays will be dealt with in an exhaustive manner later in this session. What will be discussed here will be purely perfunctory in nature.

Single dimensional Arrays The single dimensional arrays as the name suggests, handles only a single procession of similar elements. That is to say you can only have one row of elements and the size of a single dimensional array depends on the programmer.

Basically, the single dimensional arrays facilitate the accommodation of many similar elements in a single variable. More on this is discussed meticulously in the succeeding sections after which you will have a cloudless view of the single dimensional arrays Multidimensional Arrays The multidimensional arrays are two or more arrays clubbed together.

They can be of two-dimensional type or three-dimensional types or more, but you can restrict the research only to two and three dimensional arrays. An example of the two dimensional arrays is the matrix because like the matrix the two dimensional arrays have two matrices one symbolizing the row elements and the other the column elements. The three dimensional array is a shade different because the first array lists the number of tables of the two dimensional arrays. The rest of the two arrays are similar to the two-dimensional array in the sense that one is for the row and the other is for the column.

4.4. ARRAY DECLARATION

The term declaration must be quite familiar to you by now. As in your earlier endeavors at declaration, here you declare an array, i.e., the compiler should know what kind of array is to be created and of what type and size you visualize it to be. Also, when this declaration is made, it specifies to the memory that the declared amount of space has to be kept as reserve to accommodate elements of this array. The general format is as follows.

int sal [15]. The int as you know specifies the data type to the compiler and the "sal" is the variable name given to the array. Till now everything must be quite familiar. The [15] is the one to be savored. The no. 15 indicates that 16 values of the type int have to be accommodated and all of them are under the name sal. The square bracket [] indicates that the computer has encountered an array declaration. The number of square brackets increase as the dimensions of the array is increase. That is to say a two dimensional array will have two pairs of square brackets, a three-dimensional three pairs of square brackets and so on.

4.5. ARRAY INITIALIZATION

The initial step of declaring an array is done. You have given it a variable name and also declared its size but upto this stage the array is empty. It is like a school bag without any books in it. Similarly, declaration of the variable is done but some values have to be passed into it. You must be aware of initializing an ordinary variable but how do you initialize an array in which more than one value has to be initialized into one array variable. Entering data into an array: Now that you have declared an array by giving it a specific name and size you can try and explore the individualities of each element in the array, that is to say how each element is addressed in an array.

Array element indexing always starts with 0. Number[0] 1st element Number[1] 2nd element Number[2] 3rd element Number[3] 4th elementThis means that [0] will hold the first value, [1] the second, [2] the third & so on. If you want to access the fourth element of the array "sal" you have to write sal [3]. You can replace the number by using a subscript say i, a, x, etc. So, the array sal wil be written as: Sal [i] The variable i is not particular to any element but can be referred to various elements in the array one at a time.

```
for (i=0; i<=14;i++)
{
printf("enter sal");
```

```
scanf("%d, &sal[i]);
}
```

To enter the data you are using afor loop by which the number of elements entered by the user are placed in an array. When the user enters the 1st value for sal it is stored in the [0] position and then the position of the element is incremented using i++ and if any next element is entered it is placed in that position, i.e. [1]. The same process takes place till the 15th element is entered after which the condition is dissatisfied & the loop is broken. The above process of intializing is called the dynamic initialization, but it is not the only way by which the process of initializing can be undertaken.

To achieve that feat C describes two distinct methods:

i. Static initialization; and

ii. Dynamic initialization.

4.6. ACCESSING DATA FROM ARRAY

You have stored the data in an array by first initializing and then reading into an array. How do you get them out so that you can use them. Once again the for loop comes in the picture and unloads all element rather than loading as in the in the first case. You have input 15 elements in an array named sal. Suppose you want to find the sum of all the elements in the array. Follow the steps given below.

```
sum =0;
/* temporary variable */
for(i=0;i<=14;i++)
sum=sum+sal[i];
/* value of sal[i]added to sum*/ printf("sum=%f",sum);
```

The for unloads each element starting from [0]. The first time the element in the [0] position takes the place of [i] and when it is added with 0 its value is entered into sum. Next the element in the [1]st. position replaces [0]th. position and it is added to the sum which already has a computed value and a new sum is formed. This takes place until the element in the position 14 is entered into i and finally the sum is printed which has all the added values.

4.7. SIMPLE PROGRAM USING ARRAYS

```
/*array program to find average marks of 5 students */ 2.#include<stdio.h>
main()
{
int i;
int mar[5];
float avg,add=0;
for(i=0;i<=4;i++) 9.
{
printf("\nenter the marks");
scanf("%d",&mar[i]);
}
for(i=0;i<=4;i++)
add=add+mar[i];
avg=add/5;
printf("\naverage=%f",avg);
}
```

The above program is a simple example to find the average marks of 5 students once the marks are entered by the user. The array named mar is declared in line number 6 and its subscript variable is also declared The variables in which the average and the sum of the marks are to be stored is declared in line number 7 as float since they can contain decimal points The for loop is initiated in line number 8 using which the marks entered by the user will be stored in an array. Line number 11 accepts the marks from the user.

The second for loop is visible in line number 13. This for loop is for adding all the values that have been entered by the user. The addition process takes place in line 14. This and the next line is called the logic of the program. In this the first for loop takes the value which is in the [0]th position of the array and adds it with sum whose present value is 0 as initialized and this is stored in the variable add. When this is done add assumes the new value submitted to it and the old value is lost. In the next iteration the value of I is incremented and it attains the value which is in the 1st position and this is added to 'add' which already has a computed number and this added value is affixed to add which loses the previous value.

The above process is repeated until the condition is dissatisfied. The total is then divided by the number of elements, which is represented in line 15. And displayed in the subsequent output statement in line 16.

4.8. ARRAY INSIDE THE MEMORY

You must be well versed with the details of declaring, initializing, and retrieving an array. But what happens in the memory? Are the elements stored in a serial order or are they stored randomly? To answer the above queries consider on example:

int sal[5];

What are the activities that take place inside the memory when such a declaration is made? By now you must be aware of what the above statement does. The statement indicates that an array variable is to be created which is of an integer data type and the array can hold 5 elements. In the memory 10 bytes will be reserved because each integer will be 2 bytes long. Until the array is initialized with some numbers, this array will host some unrelated numbers. Once the array is initialized the elements are stored in a continuous manner.

Take a look at the tabular representation below:

2012 2014 2016 2018 2020 10 20 30–40 50

In the above table you can see that the numbers entered by the user are registered in a successive pattern and each element takes 2 bytes. This is exactly how it is represented in the memory of a computer. The number below the element location is the address of the location and each element has its unique address in the memory by which it is identified (Figure 4.1).

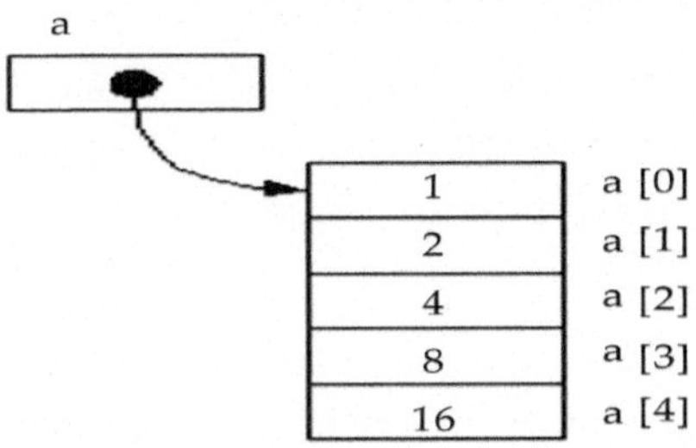

Figure 4.1. Array inside the memory.

4.9. MULTIDIMENSIONAL ARRAYS

Till now the main area of concentration has been the one-dimensional arrays. Now you enter the area of ambiguity. This statement can be argued because the multidimensional arrays are defined in a pattern that resembles the one-dimensional array. The only disparity being that the multi dimensional array requiresseparate square brackets for each subscript. That is to say if the one dimensional array had a pair of square brackets, a two dimensional array will have two pairs of square brackets, three dimensional array three pairs of square brackets, and so on.

Two Dimensional Array A two dimensional array can be visualized as an array below an array. As earlier mentioned, a two dimensional array will have two pairs of square brackets. The description can be explained as below.

Data_type array_name [expression1] [expression2];

The two dimensional array is often referred to as a matrix. The expression one and two are the subscripts that the two-dimensional array will hold. Therefore, in the above expression one will specify the row and expression, two will specify the column and they indicate the number of array elements associated with each subscript.

Therefore if a declaration states:

int arr[4][2]

It means that a two dimensional array with the name arr is of integer type and has four rows and two columns. Its representation would be like this: Column No. 0 Column No. 1 Row no. 0 1000 10 Row no. 1 2000 20 Row no. 2 3000 30 Row no. 3 4000 40. Thus the element in arr[0][0] will be 1000 and the element in arr [3][2] will be 30. The rest of the numbers can be figured by having a look at the above table. In the memory the elements are placed in a sequential pattern such that the element in [0][0] will be first followed by the element in [0][1] followed by [1][0] and so on. Here too, each integer element will occupy two bytes.

Initializing a 2 dimensional Array Initializing a two dim array is as equivalent to initializing a one-dimensional array.

int sal[4][2]={{1000,10}, {2000,20}, {3000,30} {4000,40}}

Also the initialization can be done by requesting the values from the user, the subscripts must be a variable like i, j, k, l, etc. Below is a program using the two dimensional arrays. Here the concept of matrices has been put into practice by adding two matrices. The concept of the two dimensional arrays will be explicit once you comprehend the program.

- **Example 4.1:**

/* program to add a two by two matrix */ 1. #include<stdio.h>

```
main()
{
int m1[2][2],m2[2][2],m3[2][2];
int i,j;
printf("\n Enter the first matrix \n");
for(i=0;i<2;i++)
{
for(j=0;j<2;j++)
{
scanf("%d",&m1[i][j]);
}
}
printf("\n enter the second matrix please");
for(i=0;i<2;i++)
{
for(j=0;j<2;j++)
{
scanf("%d",&m2[i][j]);
}
}
for(i=0;i<2;i++)
{
for (j=0;j<2;j++)
{
m3[i][j]=m1[i][j]+m2[i][j];
}
}
printf("\n result matrix is \n");
for(i=0;i<2;i++)
```

```
{
for(j=0;j<2;j++)
{
printf("%d",m3[i][j]);
}
printf("\n");
}
}
```

The above program will result in adding the values present in a two by two matrix with the values present in another two by two matrix. The declaration of the arrays is done in line 4 where three two dimensional arrays are declared. Two in which the values have to be inserted and added and in the third the computed value of the two matrices has to be inserted. The subscripts used are i and j As you are aware, a two dimensional array has a square bracket for row and a square bracket for column and values for each of them have to be inserted.

This is done with the help of two for loops, which are stated in lines 7 and 9. The first matrix is formed using these values. The similar process is carried out for the second matrix and the for loops are parked in lines15 and 17. Now that you have the two matrices laden with the values, these two have to be added and inserted into a third empty array. To accomplish this feat once again the for loops are summoned and they have to be present before the formula for the addition is given. These for loops are mentioned in lines22 and 24. In line 26 the logic for the program is given. Once the values are added and inserted into the third array that array has to be displayed and the output statement is explained in line 34 with the help of for statements which are in lines32 and 34. The last printf statement with a "\n" makes the result appear in a matrix format.

You must be wondering why an abundance of open and close braces are showered in the program. The braces are specified when multiple for loops is included in the program. This indicates that the statements within the braces succeeding the for loop is specific only to that particular for loop Three Dimensional Array The three dimensional array is similar to a two dimensional array. The difference being that it has an extra pair of square brackets which defines the number of tables of the matrix.

Thus, a three dimensional array is declared as follows:

```
int sal[20][25][50]
```

The above declaration indicates that the array sal is a collection of 20 tables with 25 rows and 50 columns. In this case the first element will hold post in sal[0][0][0], the second in sal[0][0][1], the third in [0][0][2] and so on. For Example: sal[10][20][30] means that the element is in the 20th row,30th column of the 10th table.

The initializing process can be depicted in the following process:

```
int sal[20][25][50]=
{
{
/*table 1*/
{1,2,3,4},
{5,6,7,8},
{9,10,11,12}
},
{
/*table 2*/
{13,14,15,16},
{17,18,19.20},
{21,22,23,24}
}
};
```

The multi dimensional arrays are processed in the same manner as the one dimensional, i.e., one element at a time. However, care should be taken when multi dimensional arrays are passed into functions. The passing of arrays into functions will be dealt with later (Figure 4.2).

	Column 0	Column 1	Column 2
Row 0	x[0][0]	x[0][1]	x[0][2]
Row 1	x[1][0]	x[1][1]	x[1][2]
Row 2	x[2][0]	x[2][1]	x[2][2]

Figure 4.2. Multi-dimensional array.

4.10. CHARACTER ARRAYS

Here is another eminent feature of the arrays, which amplifies the glory of C to endless heights. Till now you have dealt with integer arrays only but that does not imply that the boundary of an array is restricted to int's. C is so flexible that it extends its services to characters also. It means that arrays can be formed using even characters. One such array of character is called a string. A string is a collection of characters that are in a particular order.

Take a look at the initialization process in character arrays with the help of an example:

```
char name[10]= "MyDharm";
```

In the above example name is an array with an element holding capacity of 10 and it holds a string called "MyDharm." The first element is stored in the [0]th position of the array name. That is, the alphabet 'M' will be stored in the [0]th position, 'y' will be in the [1] position and so on till [9].

A doubt may arise that while the array can accommodate 10 values only 4 have been entered. What happens to the rest? Here, since only 4 values have been accommodated the 5th value will be a null character(\0) which represents the end of the string. This will be placed automatically at the end of the string if any of the array indexes are vacant. N

A blank space cannot exist between any two characters while taking input from the user unless accompanied by a specific format specifier. To accommodate the above characteristic feature the initialization should be done dynamically. Dynamic Character Initialization You have already dealt with the method of dynamic initialization early in this session. Just to refresh your memory using the initialization of the variable is done by the user through dynamic initialization, i.e., the initialization is not done in the program and the values tend to be refreshed each time the program is compiled.

This simple example explains the above:

```
/* program to accept characters from the user in an array*/
#include<stdio.h>
main()
{
char cap[10];
printf("Enter the capital of your country");
```

```
scanf("%s",cap);
printf("%s is the capital of your country",cap);
}
```

Start with line 5 since the preceding ones must be quite easy to decipher. Line 5 is where the dynamic initialization of the array takes place. It indicates to the compiler that an array is to be created which can accommodate 10 elements that are of character type. The line 7 accepts the string of characters that is entered by the user based on the display statement in line 6. Line 8 retrieves the stored string from the array and displays it back onto the screen.

Another feature of dynamic initialization of character arrays is that it facilitates the inclusion of blank spaces in between the characters of the string. This can be accomplished by altering the format specifier in the scanf statement in the following way:

```
scanf("%[^\n]", arrayname);
```

If the above statement is not specified and a blank space is even attempted to be inserted into the string the characters present after the string will be terminated without any mercy. The compiler refuses to acknowledge any characters after the blank.

4.11. ARRAY OVERFLOW

If at all any criticisms can be barraged on C it will be only in this aspect. Array over flow can be simply put as crossing the boundaries. To explain it in terms of C when an array of a particular size is declared only that many elements can be inserted into an array.

If that size limit is exceeded an error is formed which results in an irregularity in the functioning of the program and C conventionally does not check for array overflow. For example, if you declare an array like sal[10] and you enter 12 elements then an illegal operation is performed which results in an irreparable loss. Not only inserting but also accessing the element whose size is not declared is an illegal operation.

Things don't stop after an error is performed, there are possibilities that the program might be reduced to shambles. This purely depends on how significant those variables that have been overwritten are and where they are used subsequently in the program. The result of the blemish can jolt you immediately or take its toll in due course of the program. This kind of delayed revelation can be exasperating. The fact is many are misguided in this process and suspect an innocuous code that may be perfect in all measures.

The above passages may sound very disheartening and are likely to paint a dismal picture but always while using arrays just be advised in the subconscious state of the mind that arrays should never overflow. The laws of medicine holds water even in C. Prevention is better than cure.

4.12. DO'S AND DON'TS

Now that you have come to the end of this session the concept of arrays must be quite unambiguous. To help you avoid committing any errors in due course of time listed below are a few do's and don'ts which, if followed, will help you reduce errors.

- **Do's:**
  - The square brackets must be made visible besides the variable name indicating that an array has been declared, enclosing the array size.
  - Multidimensional arrays should have as many pairs of square brackets as is their number. E.g., 2pairs for 2dim arrays, 3 pairs for 3dim.
  - Initialization of the arrays is done using a loop condition.
  - If multiple for statements are used the statements succeeding it should be enclosed in a pair of braces.
- **Don'ts:**
  - The subscript value should not be negative The subscript value should not have a decimal point.
  - The subscript value should not be out of range.
  - Blank spaces should not occur in strings unless accompanied by "[^\n]" in the scanf.

4.13. SUMMARY

After the advantages of arrays, you also learnt the different subdivisions in arrays before declaring and initializing an array. A simple program was described after accessing data from the array. The internal representation of the array was depicted before moving on to multidimensional arrays which dealt with two and three dimensional arrays. The character arrays and the bounds checking for the arrays formed the concluding part of this session.

Going Over It Again:

Fill in the blanks:

1. Two or more arrays clubbed together are called ____________ arrays.
2. Arrays, element indexing always start with _________.
3. Elements in the array are stored in a ___________ manner.
4. In a three dimensional array out of the three square brackets two represent the row and the column and the third represents ___________________.
5. Initialization of the arrays is done using a ________ control structure.

State True or False:

1. The number of square brackets increase as the dimension of the array is increased.
2. Static initialization is done at the time of the declaration of the array.
3. While taking input from the user there can exist a blank space between two characters.
4. The subscript value can be negative.
5. The subscript value can be out of range.

One Line Answers:

1. What is an array?
2. What are the different types of arrays?
3. What are the different types of array initialization in C?

CHAPTER 5

Functions

Contents

5.1. INTRODUCTION TO FUNCTIONS

You are about to enhance your skills in yet another feather in C's cap for which an introduction of just about half a page will be depriving it of its merits. The reason why it is being emphasized to such an extent is because if you thought arrays was incomparable the mere shadow of functions will give arrays a run for its money and this is not an exaggeration, because arrays was a concept but functions is a saga of its own which has a chronicle of merits to its credit. It is like the flute, which the pied piper played, the armory of cupid, without which any of the stipulated operations cannot be performed.

One just can't imagine writing a C program without having a function. It's just not possible. Once you adopt the functions you will realize the amount of solace you experience in a true friend like the functions, in the sense that it simplifies your job. It performs the task that you order it to do. It is similar to hiring a specific person to do a specific job.

For example you rely on the electrician to fix up blown fuses or the carpenter to install the kitchen cabinets. In a similar way the functions perform the tasks allotted to them with immaculate perfection. It is as elegant and perfect as the live concert of Beethoven. How do Functions perform? The functions in C are generally used by C whenever a particular set of instructions have to be executed more than once during the course of the program. Say a particular section of the code finds out the average marks of the students of class 8. Later the average for class 10 also has to be found out.

It is not necessary to write the same code once again. It is like inventing the wheel. The code can be written in a function and can be used each time by just altering the values.

How this feat can be pulled off is when a code is written in a function (how this is done is dealt later) that particular function can be called anywhere in the program by mentioning the function name followed by the parentheses, e.g., sub() This is termed calling of a function. Adopting functions proves to be an added asset because functions are easy to code and understand apart from being easier to debug. That is to say finding out the errors is easy due to the simple compact nature of the functions and the errors are more apparent.

Also programs containing functions are easier to maintain because modifications if required are restricted to certain functions. If you think that this was too much listen to this. The functions can be deposited in a library which contains similar functions printf(), scanf() and they can be recalled by any and many programs.

5.2. ADVANTAGES OF FUNCTIONS

What you have skimmed through above, is just a general idea of the functions and the kind of operations they perform. Listed below are a few of the merits the functions offer to the programmer and more often than not the programmers comply with the functions and find that the pains of programming if any, are alleviated. A programmer can exploit the below mentioned advantages to the fullest and reap the rich rewards of implementing functions.

A programmer can identify whatever actions are performed repeatedly in various parts of the program, write them as a function and call the function from various parts of the program, wherever needed. This approach avoids code duplication. Instead of duplicating the same code in different parts of the program, you just write the function once and call it from different parts of the program, thus reducing the executable file size and redundancy of code, making the maintenance of code easy.

In multitasking systems like Unix, there is a direct relationship between the amount of memory a program consumes and the speed with which it runs. You will, in general find that large programs which demand a lot of memory, are sluggish.

Breaking down your program into subroutines lends your program a structure. You can divide you task into multiple sub-tasks, develop a function for each sub-task, and integrate them into a single program. Once a function is written and completely tested, a programmer can expect it to smoothly fit in with the rest of the program modules.

Once a function is written, tested, and found to be working as per the expectations, the function can be loaded into a library, and can be used in an altogether different application. This approach encourages code reusability.

5.3. DECLARING A FUNCTION

After reading the prologue about functions you must be waiting anxiously and expectantly to kick start and get into the thick of things. You will no longer be kept on hold and will now start by declaring a function which is one of the basic bricks in the structure of a function.

You may ask why declare a function at all. The reason is obvious and same as done for earlier concepts declaration. The compiler has to be aware that a function is being defined and whenever the need arises for the function to perform its execution, it should revert to the function where it is defined. It is like whenever the fuse blows the electrician is summoned and he performs his duty. The basic and the first function you encounter while writing a program is the main function. Within this main function the rest of the sub functions are defined and called. It is like there are four concentric circles and the outer most circle encompasses the rest of the inner circles.

The main function can be compared with the outer most circle and the sub functions the inner circles. A C program can exist without a sub function but a C program cannot exist without a main function which as you know encloses the body of the program. The declaration process is a two-step procedure. The first being the function and argument declaration and the second the implementation or the body of the function.

Function and Argument Declaration This forms the first line of the function and is formatted generally in the following way.

```
data type function_name (type1 arg1,type2 arg2)
{
statement 1;
statement 2;
}
```

The data type preceding the function name is specific for the function and specifies to the compiler the type of element that will be returned by the function (i.e., int, char) as the answer. If you take a peek inside the parentheses you might seem puzzled but what happens is that arguments to be passed to the function must be declared along with their data type.

Arguments are nothing but the variables that we are familiar with. It is just that these arguments or variables are declared locally or to say they are valid only within that particular function in which they are declared. The function name along with the parameters if any are mentioned wherever you want the control to execute the code in the function.

The compiler on encountering the function call transfers the control to the function definition. The function name with the parentheses which transfers the control is the caller function and the function name under which the body of the function is present is the called function. If there is still a cloud of doubts they dispelled will be blown away with the help of this example. To maintain simplicity no arguments are included.

```
#include<stdio.h>
main()
{
tips();
\*caller*\
printf("\n Success is about hanging on after others have let go");
}
tips()
\*called*\
{
printf("\nWhen you reach the end of the rope tie a knot & hang on");
}
```

The above program is a simple example which will help you take a whiff of the actual happenings. In this program soon after the main function the function called tips is invoked or called. As soon as this happens the control is passed on to the place where the function tips is defined.

Once the control reaches the called function it executes the statements within that function and returns to the caller function and executes the statements after it. So, the output of the above program would be:

When you come to the end of the rope tie a knot & hang on. Success is about hanging on when others have let go.

5.4. CALLING A FUNCTION

The intricacies of declaring a function were just explained in detail but what use is it if you just declare a function and don't call it. Hence you will now deal with the process of calling a C function. You have defined the function but how do you summon the compiler to execute the code in the function definition? Well, you just call it. Calling in the sense you give some kind of indication or to put it clearly a kind of arrow sign which requests the compiler to take diversion and carry on further execution from the place specified.

The compiler, when it encounters this sign. passes the control to the function definition and executes the statements in the function. It can be compared with the goto statements of the control structures. Whenever the goto statements were encountered, the control used to transfer itself to the place indicated. These indicators which inform the compiler to change direction are called the caller functions and the functions definition where the control passes is known as the called function. A function in C can be accessed or called by specifying its name followed by the list of arguments, i.e., variables with corresponding data types enclosed in the parentheses and each of them distinctly separated by commas. The inclusion of the arguments is dependent on the nature of the function. That is there are some function which don't pass arguments just like the one you dealt with in the earlier unit. If such is the case, then the function name is followed by a pair of empty parentheses.

The arguments if any, passed in the caller functions are termed as actual arguments and the arguments passed in the first line of the function of definition is termed as formal arguments. The arguments can be thought of as a means of transportation for the values used in the program. The values in the form of variables are transported from the main function where they are declared to the sub function where they are utilized.

Once the values are utilized for the computation and the result is found out the computed result is returned to the caller function if required. The actual arguments maybe expressed as constants, single variables or more complex expressions. However, the important thing to note is that the data type integrity of both the actual arguments and the formal arguments must be maintained the same. Another important fact is that there can be different calls to the same function from various places in the program, just like many computer terminals are connected to a single server. The actual arguments may differ from one function called to another, but the numbers, arguments, and the data type of the arguments must be maintained the same and in the same order or else it can result in an error causing disruption of the program. Hence care has to be taken while calling a function.

5.5. VARIABLES

Variables by this time you must be playing with variables in your program melting and moulding them as per your requirement. The spotlight will how be focussed on how these variables behave inside a function and what type of variables fall in place for what type of declaration. Before taking off on these issues you should be aware of the different kinds of variables that exist in C's arsenal. The types of variables being the: Local Variables Global Variables Local Variables You are aware of the fact that main is a function and you can declare any number of variables within it. So, if a rule holds good for one function why cant it for other functions? It definitely can.

You can declare a variable inside any function belonging to any size and type. Thus, variables declared inside a function are called local variables and are valid and can be used within that function. The life of these variables exists until they are within the function. It is same, as the value of a particular variable in a program cannot exist for all the programs.

Any attempt to break the rules will result in an error. But sometimes you might need to access the variable from another function, well C takes care of this too. The values can be imported from other functions by passing them in parameters. But with passing parameters care should be taken that the same number of variables and the same type are being passed. Thus, a copy of the actual parameters is made and passed to the formal parameters. All this is an extra burden and is cumbersome for the programmer. Beside this, several functions are required to share information, which results in transmission and re-transmission of parameters, which affect the performance of the program. The value in the variables if altered in a sub-function does not affect the value is the main function.

Global Variable Before you can accuse C of being inefficient in certain areas it pops up with an alternative. The alternative for reducing the afore mentioned problem is declaring the variables globally. You were given an example of the global declarations in the first session. The global variables are otherwise called external variables and unlike the local variables which are confined only to the function which has them, the global variables can be used anywhere in the program. The global variables are declared outside the main, i.e., before beginning the program and the values hold good throughout the program. The storage for global variables is in a fixed region of memory set aside for this specific purpose by the C compiler.

The effectiveness of declaring globally can be felt when many functions in a program use the same data. Defining a variable as global is particularly advantageous because its value is made available to all other functions. But the only risk factor involved in this is that if any function manipulates or alters the global variable then any other function using the same variable at the same time gets the altered value. So, the choice of using global variables has to be made judiciously considering the above implication.

5.6. PASSING ARGUMENTS TO A FUNCTION

You have been informed about the arguments and about the passing of arguments earlier, but if you feel that the concepts were unclear then this section of the session will set things right. Here you will not only be clear about what arguments are but also you will be getting acquainted with the types of functions based on the arguments passed.

The concepts of passing arguments in a function just make it more compatible to use, the reason being that the arguments acts as a medium of communication between the caller and the called function. You might have been ignorant about the fact that you have used arguments when you dealt with the plethora of printf and scanf functions. The matter, which you specified within the parentheses, is considered as arguments. The types of function based on the arguments passed to them is mentioned below:

- Functions which don't take parameters and do not return any value.
- Functions which accepts parameters but do not return any value.
- Functions which take parameter and returns values.

Each of the above types will be taken up individually so that you will get more than an over view of the types of functions that are available in the C arsenal. Functions which do not take parameters and do not return any value. For functions of this type neither the caller function nor the called function take any arguments.

What happens here is that when a function is called the control jumps directly to the called function and executes the statements that are specified within the called function. After the statements in the called function are executed, the control returns to the main program.

Example:

```
main()
{
mus();
}
mus()
{
printf("My Honey");
}
```

In the above simple program once the control encounters the caller functions in this case mus() the control directs itself to the called function and executes the statements and executes the printf statement below it and returns to the main. In this case the result of a program would be:

5.6.1. My Honey

Functions that accepts parameters but don't return values. For functions this the caller function transport, some values to the called function or the function definition where these values are used for some specific function or computation but once the computed value is found out within the called function the value is not returned back to the caller function.

The program below should give a clear picture.

- **Example:**

```
main()
{
int a,b; printf("Enter a & b");
scanf("%d %d", &a,&b);
add (a,b);
}
add(intx,inty)
{
int z;
z=x+y;
printf("a+b=%d", z);
clrscr();
}
```

In the above event once the values are passed into the called function they are summed up and the total is displayed within the function itself. Functions that takes parameters and returns values In the third & final type of functions the values as the arguments are being passed into the called function where they will be computed and a definite result is relayed back to the caller function and the value will be printed from there. The following things should comprehend things further:

```
#include<stdio.h>
```

```
main()
{
int a,b,ans;
printf("Enter a");
scanf("%d", &a);
printf("enter b");
scanf("%d",&b);
ans=add(a,b);
printf("the addition of two numbers is %d",ans);
}
add(x,y)
int x,y;
{
int z;
z=x+y;
return(z);
}
```

The above program, is similar to the earlier one barring that in this program the result after being computed is returned back to the caller function and it is printed from there.

5.7. A SIMPLE PROGRAM USING FUNCTIONS

After acknowledging the different aspects of functions in C namely knowing how to declare a function and pass arguments into the function and also being aware of the process of calling a function it seems fair enough to start writing your first program in functions which will be using all the aspects that have been encompassed in the earlier units of this session.

Below is a program which computes the factorial of any given number.

```
/*program to compute the factorial of a given number*/ 2.#include<stdio.
h>
main()
{
```

```
int a,f;
printf("\nEnter any number");
scanf("%d",&a);
f=fact(a);
printf("Factorial value=%d",f);
}
fact(int x)
{
int prod=1,i;
for(i=1;i<=x;i++)
prod=prod*i;
return(prod);
}
```

The values to be passed into the functions are declared at the declaration depot at the beginning of the program. The request from the user is made in line 6 using the printf and the number is accepted using the scanf which is displayed in the 7th line The caller function fact is visible in the 8th line which passes the argument being the number entered by the user. In the same line that function is assigned to a variable f in which the returned value is dumped. This value is then printed using the printf statement which is specified in line number 9. The called function is given in line number 11 in which the value entered by the user is passed on using the variable x. It is highly essential that the data type of the variable must be specified adjacent to the variable within the parentheses. In line number 13 the local declaration of the variables that are to be used within that particular function is done. In this case prod and i are declared locally. The for loop structure is specified in line number 14. In the for the value of i is initialized to one and the condition is set that the loop should continue until the value of i reaches that of the number entered by the user and it is incremented. The logic to find the factorial specified in line number 15 were the prod is multiplied with value in i and it is entered in prod so when the value of i is incremented it is multiplied with the new value of prod. This process continues until the condition is satisfied. Once the final value of prod that is the factorial of the given number is found out it is returned to the caller function, the procedure for which is specified in line number 16.

5.8. NESTED FUNCTIONS

The word nested must be familiar to you because you have been earlier acclimatized with the nested ifelse statement and also the nested loops. The nested functions are no different to the earlier ones, the change being that here the functions are being nested or one function is called from within another function. Nesting of functions in simpler terms can be thought of as calling a function from within a function. The parent function calls the child sub-functions each of them after computing a result returns their values to the parent function if required. You cannot define a function within another function, you can call a function from another function.

- **Example 5.1:**

```
#include<stdio.h>
main()
{
nest();
call();
}
nest()
{
call();
}
call()
{
printf("\n when you are at crossroads, make a fifth one of your own");
}
```

In the above program the functions are called in lines 4 and 5. When the control encounters the function nest it jumps to the function definition to line number 7 and within that function it encounters the nested function call and further jumps to the function definition of the call and executes the statements in that function.

5.9. PASSING ARRAY TO FUNCTIONS

The dealings with passing arguments in a function must have looked like child's play to you so here is a concept that tends to make life difficult for you. Since you have been dealing with arrays in the previous session, the concept must be pretty fresh in your minds. Well here is just a tester.

You will now try to pass on an array into a function or to be specific the array elements have to the passed into a function so that they can be used in that function. To pass an array to a function, the first thing to be done is to declare the array before it can be used in the function.

This can be done as you know at the declaration depot after the main function. To pass an array to a function the array name should be without the square bracket or subscript in the actual parameter, i.e., in the caller function. In the corresponding called function the formal argument must have an array name with the square bracket which is empty. The rough example given below should take care of things.

```
main()
{
int a,sub[20];
statements;
statements;
sal(a,sub)
\*caller*\
statements statements
}
float sal(int a,int x[])
\*called*\
{
statements
}
```

- **Example:**

```
#include<stdio.h>
main()
{
int i;
int sub[]={10,20,30,40,50,60,70};
for(i=0;i<=6;i++)
```

```
disp(sub[i]);
}
disp(int a)
{
printf("%d\n",a);
}
```

The program depicted above is simple program which displays the effective use of passing arrays into a function. The declaration and the initialization is done in line number 5 where the elements are initialized in a static mode. Line number 6 is for entering the elements of the array into the variable that is to be passed into the called function. This is done using a for loop and the subscript attached to it is i. The caller function is visible in line number 7 where the function name is accompanied by the array name within the parentheses with the square bracket along with the subscript. When the control encounters the caller function it transfers itself to the place where the function is defined. The called function is given in line number 9 along with a variable which transfers the values of the array into the function.

The values once entered into the function through the variable are displayed within the function using the printf statement in line number 11. Hence the output of the program would be as follows:

10 20 30 40 50 60 70

5.10. RECURSION IN FUNCTIONS

Recursion in general terms means repeating itself. But how does that apply to a function? A recursive function is a process where the function calls itself repeatedly until a particular condition is satisfied. It is more like the loop conditions discussed in session – 3. But the difference lies in that each action or recursion is based in the result of the previous one. A recursive result triggers the recursive action for the next result until the condition is satisfied. For a problem to be solved recursively there are 2 conditions to be satisfied.

The problem must be written in a recursive form. The recursion must have a condition which seals the recursion. We have discussed the factorial program earlier in the session. Let us now find the factorial of any given number using recursion. Though it looks very tiny and innocuous don't get taken in by the books.

```
#include<stdio.h>
main()
{
int a,fact;
printf("\nEnter any number");
scanf("%d",&a);
fact=rec(a);
printf("Factorial value is%d",fact);
}
rec(x)
int x;
{
int f;
if(x==1)
return(1);
else
f=x*rec(x-1);
return(f);
}
```

For your better comprehension the example of the factorial which was discussed earlier is taken to explain the concept of recursion. You must understand this recursive factorial function thoroughly. In the first run when the number entered through scanf() is 1, just observe what action does rec() take. The value of a (i.e., 1) is copied into x. Since x turns out to be 1 the condition if (x == 1) is satisfied and hence 1 is returned through the return statement. When the number entered through scanf() is 2, the (x == 1) test fails, so you reach the statement.

f= x*rec(x–1);

And here is where you meet recursion. How can you best handle the expression x*rec(x-1). You multiply x by rec(x–1). Since the current value of x is 2, it is same as saying that you must calculate the current (2*rec (1)). You know that the value returned by rec (1) is 1, so the expression reduces to (2 *1), or simply 2.

Thus the statement x * rec(x–1);

Thus the statement evaluates to 2, which is stored in the variable f, and is returned to main(), where it is duly printed as.

Factorial value is 2.

5.11. CALL BY VALUE AND CALL BY REFERENCES

After all that grilling of the technicalities used in function and the methods utilized you must be thorough with the concepts and technicalities about how to call a function in C. When you crammed the concepts of passing arguments in your mind you have passed only values into the function. Knowingly or unknowingly what you have done is termed as call by value in C technical jargon. To recapitulate, after declaring the variables you passed the values into the function through these variables sub(x, y);

You have also been apprised that once you declare a variable and assign a value to it the value is stored at some place in the memory. Just out of curiousness one might ask without having to touch the values if it is possible to send the values through the address. The answers is "yes" and it is termed as call by reference, i.e., you are taking the reference of the address to send the value. So, you have two ways of passing arguments.

Call by value Call by reference Call by Value In this process the variables are declared and initialized with a value before being passed. But once they are passed into the function you decide it's an unlucky number and you don't like that number to exist in the sub function and you change the values of the variable. Eventhough the values are changed inside the sub function they are undeterred in the main:

```
/*program using functions to interchange two values*/ 1.#include<stdio.h>
main()
{
int x=2,y=3;
ichange(x,y);
printf("\nthe old value of x=%d",x);
printf("\nthe old value of y=%d",y);
}
ichange(int i,int j)
{
```

```
int k;
k=i;
i=j;
j=k;
printf("\n the new value of x=%d",i);
printf("\n the new value of y=%d",j);
}
```

The output of the above program would be as follows:

The new value of x = 3

The new value of y = 2

The old value of x = 2

The old value of y = 3

The above program explains clearly that even though if the values in the function are altered they are not affected in the main program the program is about swapping the values of two variables. In the sense that variables are initialized with a particular number but their values are inter changed in the program. The declaration part in line number 4 specifies that the values of x and y are 2 and 3 respectively. The variables are then transferred to the called function by specifying them in the caller function which is in line number 5. The control then passes to the called function where they will be utilized. The called function is specified in line number 9. Within the function a third variable k is declared and the variables of x and y are changed to i and j. Such a thing will not cause any alternation the values of the variables and is perfectly valid.

Line number 12, 13, 14, is logic of swapping the two values. What happens here is that the value of I that is 2 is submitted to k and the values of j that is 3 is submitted to I so the present value of i is 3. In line number 14 the value of k that is 2 is submitted to j and the new value of j becomes 2. Thus, the two values are swapped. The new values of I and j are printed in line number 15 and 16.

Once this is done the control returns back to the caller function and executes the statements below that if any. You can see in the output that the new values of x and y will be displayed as 3 and 2 respectively but once control goes back to the main function the old values remain the same as initialized in the beginning. Thus, you can see that though the values are altered in the called function once the control returns to the program, the new values are lost and the old value are used once again.

Call by Reference Try the above thing here and you will end up losing the previous value. Why? Because you are using the addresses of the arguments and any tampering with the values would result in erasing the old value from the address and installation of the new address.

```
#include<stdio.h>
main()
{
int a=10,b=20;
ichange(&a,&b); printf("\na=%db=%d",a,b);
}
ichange(int *x,int *y)
{
int t; t=*x; *x=*y; *y=t;
}
```

The above program is similar to the one dealt with before, i.e., the swapping of two numbers. The difference being that earlier values were being used but in the above program instead of values the address of the value from the memory is used to swap the two values and hence once the control returns to the program the new values are retained.

5.12. DO'S AND DON'TS

As usual at the end of the session you should be aware of the rules of the game. So, here are a few do's and don'ts that have to be followed religiously while implementing functions.

- **Do's:**
  - A function can be called any number of times.
  - The order in which the functions are defined in a program and the order in which they get called need not necessarily be same.
  - A function can call itself. Such a process is called *recursion.*
  - A function can be called from other function,
  - The caller function should be terminated with a semicolon.

- **Don'ts:**
  - A function cannot be defined in another function.
  - Do not change the data type of the variables between the caller and the called function.
  - The program cannot start without a function. The mandatory one being the main()

5.13. SUMMARY

In this session you learnt the means and methods of declaring and calling a function after which the various types of variables used in the functions were discussed. A simple program using functions was developed after learning the techniques of argument passing. The earlier session was revisited by learning how to pass an array into a function. Towards the concluding parts the call by value and the call by reference and the recursion in functions was discussed.

Going Over It Again:

Fill in the blanks:

1. The process of declaration is a _________ step procedure.
2. The function name under which the body of the function is present is called the _________ function.
3. Arguments passed in the caller function are termed as __________ arguments.
4. After the statements in the called function are executed the control returns to the _________.
5. The method by which the values can be passed using the address is called___________.

CHAPTER 6

Pointers

Contents

6.1. INTRODUCTION TO POINTERS

All through your journey with C you have been sailing with the goodies of C and it's time now to meet the bad boys. The journey from here will be extremely interesting but at the same time, very challenging. Till now you had been reading comics but now you will get to read some serious stuff that will change your total approach towards the game. This is in no way meant to startle you but to counsel you that your mindset has to undergo a transformation from a boyish attitude to a more mature one because you will encounter a plethora of the technical jargon used in C. There is one aspect that differentiates a good C programmer from a novice.

The pointers Some programmers dread to use the pointers and that's why the hot seat eludes them. But then you must be thinking why jitters are being given even before the definition is explained. Well it's not to alarm you but to just apprise you of the significance of pointers in C. The reason why pointers may be a shade trickier than the rest of the is because their operations are entirely behind the screen, i.e., in the memory and it is always complex to comprehend the internals of the computer.

After reading the brief prologue about pointers you must be raring to have your first dash with pointers. According to the definition a pointer is a data type which can have a variable that represents the location of a data item like an integer. The effectiveness of pointers is admirable because pointers can be used to pass information back and forth between a function and its reference point. Before you even set your hands on pointers there is one basic brick that has to be comprehended and that is the address. You might ask address of what? What happens is whenever any variable is declared and stored in the memory it is assigned a particular location. Just like when you check into a hotel you are allotted a particular suite from the multitude of rooms which has a unique number specific to only that. Whenever any reference is to be made, it is done so using that unique number. In a similar way the location in which the variable is stored has a unique number which is called the address of the variable and any reference to the variable is done through this address. Note The address of any variable is always a whole number.

6.2. POINTERS – THE BEGINNING

The first question that can come to your mind when speaking about pointers is what exactly is pointers? Pointer as defined earlier, nothing but just another data type of C. That is to say it is just like int, char, float. Pointers are the most effective of the data types present in C because they have direct dealings with the memory that to say it points to a particular address in the memory.

Let us consider once again the internal structure of a variable declaration by considering the following example: int x=5. When this is done you know that a variable is associated with an integer with a value 5 and some space in the memory must be kept aside for storing it.

The internal representation can be depicted as below:

x 3456.

Above you will notice that the computer has allotted the memory location with the number 3456 to store the number 5. This number 3456 is the address of x where its value 5 is stored and whenever the program has to recall the value of x from the memory it uses the number 3456 to identify where its value is stored.

The point to be grasped here is that the & and * operator. All this while you have been using the above operators for different purposes. The & operator was used in the scanf() statements to accept the number entered by the user but here the & operator has a different function altogether.

By using this operator before any variable in the printf() statements the address of that particular variable is displayed.

printf("Address of i=%d", &i);

The above printf() statements prints the address value of i.

Address of i=8349. The other operator which you were introduced to was the * operator which was used by you as arithmetic operator of multiplication. But in pointer jargon it is called value at address operators. As the term suggests when this operator is used along with variable and its address symbol (&), the value which is present at the address of that particular variable is displayed.

printf("value of i=%d",*(&i));

The output would be as below:

Value of i = 5

In the above example you can see that the * is used outside the parentheses within which is enclosed the address of i? Note Printing the value of *(&i) is as equivalent as printing the value of i.

6.3. POINTER VARIATIONS

You will now dig deep into the different pointer variations that are up on offer. There are basically three types of pointer variations that are described by C.

They are:

- Pointer declaration;
- Pointer arithmetic;
- Pointer comparisons.

Each of the above variations has a story to tell but the discussion will be limited to what is pertaining to your up gradation of knowledge about pointers. Pointer Declaration If you are thinking that this is yet another declaration, this is nowhere remotely near the earlier ones.

The pointer declaration or it can be called pointer assignment, is where the address of a particular variable is assigned or initialized to another variable. That is to say the value of a variable will be the address of another variable. Consider the following example x=&y; In the above depiction the address of y is the value of x that is, if the address of y is 2457 and the assignment is done then the value of x will also be 2457.

But the variable x has to be declared before it can actually be used. If there is still a doubt in your mind the graphic representation below should erase it. Address of x, y is 8123 and 2457.

If the addresses have to be entered into a variable the variable should be declared in a particular manner after the main. Take a look below. 2457 5 int *x; That is how the pointer variables are declared. The above declaration tells the compiler that the variable x is being used to store an address of another variable and thus variables declared of this type can be used only to store addresses and nothing else. These are called pointer variables and each pointer variable should be preceded by a * operator along with the specification of data type.

Pointer Arithmetic When referring to arithmetic your area of concern will be to study if arithmetic can be incorporated into the concept of pointers and if yes to what extent is arithmetic valid in pointers. It is sad declaring the fact that in pointers only addition and subtraction operations can be performed and apart from this nothing else.

6.3.1. Addition

The addition operation can be performed effectively using pointers in a way that addition of a number to a pointer is possible.

- **Example:**

```
#include<stdio.h>
void main()
{
int i=4,*x,*y;
x=&i;
y=x+9;
printf("%d",y);
}
```

The above example is a rough program. You can see that x and y are declared as pointer variables and i is initialized to 4. The next step being that the address of i is assigned to x and the value of x is added 9 and placed in the variable y which is printed in the next line. In a similar way, subtraction using pointers can also be accomplished. **y=x-9;**

6.3.2. Pointer Comparison

The comparison between pointer variable can be done provided both the variables point to the objects of same data type. Such comparisons can be useful when both pointer variables point to the elements of the same array. The comparison can test for either equality or inequality and also a Pointer variable can be compared with zero.

The program below gives us a description of how its is carried out.

```
#include<stdio.h>
void main()
{
static int sub[]={10,20,30,40,50,60};
int *a,*b; a=&sub[4]; b=(sub+4);
if(a==b)
printf("pointers point to the same location.");
else
```

```
printf("They do not point");
}
```

6.4. DYNAMIC MEMORY ALLOCATION

Remember that in arrays you faced a problem of array overflow. That is if the number of elements exceeded the size declared by you in the array, it would result in the program causing an illegal function and result in a runtime error. To be more clear if you declared an array like [15] and after you entered 15 elements you realize you require 20 elements to be stored, storing the extra elements at that point of time would be impossible in arrays. On the other hand you have declared the size over abundantly and while execution you don't require that much space and if retained it will result in eating up all your storage space.

The above hindrances can be rectified successfully using the dynamic memory allocation, which is called the malloc() and calloc(). These are basically standard library functions and they produce memory instantly on the spot during execution time. The malloc function is used to allocate memory at run time and when a malloc is called it is accompanied by only one parameter in the parentheses which specifies the number of bytes of memory required.

The malloc can be asked to allocate space for any data type that int, char, float. The other type of dynamic memory allocation is the calloc() which is also a library function the difference between malloc being that when malloc takes only argument in the parentheses the calloc takes 2 arguments within the parentheses. The other major difference between these then is that where calloc initializes the allotted space to zeros, malloc does not provide any initialization and the space allocated by malloc will contain only garbage values until a number is entered. Thus, by using these 2 functions memory can be allocated at run time after clearly determining the size of the input.

- **Example 6.1:**

```
#include<stdio.h>
#include<malloc.h>
#include<stdlib.h>
void main()
{
int a, avg, *i,*c, add = 0;
```

```
printf("Enter the number of students ");
scanf("%d", &a);
c=(int*) malloc (a *2);
if (c = = NULL)
{
printf("\nMemory allocation not possible");
exit(0)
}
for (i=c; i<(c+a);i++)
scanf ("%d",i);
for (i=c;i<(c+a);i++)
{
add = add +(*i);
}
avg=add/a;
printf("Average marks = %d", avg);
}
```

Here, we first ask for the number of students whose marks are to be entered and then allocate only as much memory as is really required to store these mark. Not a byte more, not a byte less. The allocation job is done by malloc(). It returns a NULL if memory allocation is unsuccessful. If successful it returns the address of the memory chunk that was allocated. This address you collected in an integer pointer c.

The expression (int*) is used to type cast the address being returned as the address of an integer rather than a character. This type casting is necessary since malloc() by default returns a pointer to a void. In the first for loop using simple pointer arithmetic you store the marks entered from the keyboard into the memory that has been allocated. In the second for loop you access the same values and sum them up to find the average marks.

6.5. POINTERS AND ARRAYS

A distinct bond seems to exist between arrays and functions. Both seem to be made for each other in the sense that a pointer can be treated as though it were an array and vice versa. A pointer can be treated as an array and indexed across if an only if it is presently pointing to an array.

Consider the following:

```
#include<stdio.h>
void main()
{
static char arr[15]="MyDharm";
char *a = "MyDharm";
printf ("%s\n", arr);
printf("%s", a);
}
```

Here even though the declarations of arr and a are different the output of both the printf statement is the same. In the 1st declaration "MyDharm" is stored in the array arr []; but in the second "MyDharm" is stored in some place in the memory and the base address is stored in a in other words a points to the 0th element in the string.

6.6. POINTERS TO POINTERS

This concept is just the extensibility of pointer. Pointer as you know is a variable that contains the address of a variable. But if a pointer variable has to store the address of another pointer variable. (This is possible only in pointers.) the declaration pattern is slightly altered. The variable which stores the address of another variable is declared with a* before it (*i) and if the pointer variable has to store the address of another pointer variable that variable will have two *, i.e., (**) followed by the variable. Observe how the variables are declared.

```
int a; int *b; int **c;
```

Here a is an ordinary int, b is a pointer to an int whereas *c is a pointer to an int pointer. This declaring of pointer to pointer must be quite lucid to you. Try to comprehend the example given next page.

```
#include<stdio.h>
void main()
{
int a =3;
int*b; 6. int**c;
```

```
b=&a;
c=&b;
printf("Address of a =%d=n",&a);
printf("Address of a =%d=n",&b);
printf("Address of a =%d=n",&*c);
printf("Address of b =%d=n",&b);
printf("Address of b=%d=n",&*c);
printf("Address of c=%d=n",&c);
printf("Value of b=%d\n",b);
printf("Value of c=%d\n",c);
printf("Value of a=%d\n",a);
printf("Value of a=%d\n",*(&a));
printf("Value of a=%d\n",*b);
printf("Value of a=%d\n",**c);
}
```

The output of the above program would be: Address

Address of a=9876

Address of a =9876

Address of b =8765

Address of b =8765

Address of c =7654

Value of b =9876

Value of c =8765

Value of a =5

Value of a =5

Value of a =5

Value of a =5

Would help you in tracing out how the program prints the above output. a b c 5 9876 8765 9876 8765 7654.

6.7. POINTERS TO FUNCTIONS

In the earlier session you had a great deal of discussion about functions and their different types So here is functions once again. You know that variables have addresses, which can be displayed, or be transferred to a pointer variable. But can this be done with a pointer? Yes it can be done because in C even functions have addresses and you can even assign that value to another pointer variable but let us go slow and first discuss how can you find the address of a function.

Observe and analyze the program below.

```
#include<stdio.h>
main()
{
int disp();
printf("The address of function is %d",disp);
disp();
}
disp()
{
printf{"Ever heard of auntie viruses?");
}
```

The output would be:

The address function is 3152

Ever heard of auntie viruses.

To display the address of the function all you have to do is give the function name in the printf statements and the function should be declared along with the data type. Now that you know how to invoke the address of a function let's proceed and learn how to assign these addresses to pointer variables.

```
#include<stdio.h>
void main()
{
int disp();
int (*fun_ptr)();
```

```
fun_ptr=disp;
printf("address is %d",fun_ptr);
(*fun_ptr)();
}
disp()
{
printf("aliens are tasty");
}
```

The output of the program would be:

address is 5211

aliens are tasty.

You must be bewildered after encountering the declaration int(*fun-ptr) (); Well take it as a rule that this is how a pointer into which the address of a function is to be passed should be written. The rest of the program must be easy to comprehend.

6.8. FUNCTIONS RETURNING POINTERS

You must be wondering why the functions have been reincarnated. The reason is that these concepts cannot be explained unless the knowledge of pointers is adequate. Now that pointers to some extent have entered your veins be advised that functions can not only return values back to the caller function but also pointers can be returned from within the called function. However, certain rules have to be incorporated to achieve such a feat. To make a function return a pointer it has to be explicitly mentioned in the calling function as well as the function declaration. The following program illustrates this.

```
#include<stdio.h>
void main()
{
int *a; int *func();
a=func();
printf("value of A is",a);
}
int *func()
```

```
{
int x=13; return(&x);
}
```

In this program the address of i is initialized and declared in the called function and returned to the caller function which is assigned p and the value of p on the address of i is displayed using the printf statements.

6.9. TWO-DIMENSIONAL ARRAYS AND POINTERS

You have already been apprised about the 2 dimensional arrays in the session Arrays and you are aware that a 2dimensional array has a row and a column and it is usually a matrix. Here you will be acquainted with the representation of the 2 dimensional array with respect to a pointer.

A 2 dimensional array is actually an assortment of 1 dimensional arrays. Therefore, one can define a two dimensional array as a pointer to a group of contiguous 1 dimensional arrays.

The general format can be specified as follows. data _type (*ptrvar) [size]; According to the above format data type refers to the data type of the array, ptrvar is the name of the pointer variable. Notice the parentheses that surround the array name and the preceding asterisk in the pointer version of each declaration.

These parentheses must be present. Without them you would be defining an array of pointers rather than a pointer to a group of arrays, since these particular symbols (i.e., the square brackets and the asterisk) would normally be evaluated right to left.

- **Example 6.2:**

```
int (*a)[20];
```

In this a is defined to be a pointer to a group of contiguous, one-dimensional, 20-element integer arrays. Thus, a points to the first 20-element array, which is actually the first row (i.e., row 0) of the original two-dimensional array.

Similarly. (a + 1) points to the second 20-element array, which is the second row (row – 1) of the original two dimensional array, and so on, as illustrated below.

a (a + 1)

6.10. ARRAY OF POINTERS

You have already dealt with a means of storing a number of elements in single variable using arrays. So, it would not be difficult to store a number of addresses using arrays. This is called an array of pointers which means a collection of addresses. It can be visualized as a telephone directory which stores many telephone numbers sequentially and whenever needed any address can be retrieved. The addresses present in the array of pointer can contain addresses of isolated variables or addresses of array elements. The following example should clear things.

```
#include<stdio.h>
void main()
{
int*sub[4];
int a=11,b=12,c=13,d=14,e;
sub[0]= &a;
sub[1]= &b;
sub[2]= &c;
sub[3]= &d;
for (e=0;e<3;e++);
printf("%d",*/sub[e]));
}
```

In the above program you will notice that once the variables and array are declared and initialized, the address of each variable is stored in the array starting from 0 for the first element. The for loop picks up the addresses present in sub and prints the values present at these addresses. An array of pointers is very famous for storing several strings in the memory. The addresses of these strings can be stored in an array of pointers.

6.11. EXTRAS ON POINTER DECLARATIONS

Before computing this chapter we mention that pointer declarations can become complicated, and some care is required in their interpretation. This is especially true of declaration that involve functions or arrays. Once difficulty is the dual use of parentheses. In particular, parentheses are used to indicate functions, and they are used for nesting purposes (to establish precedence) with in more complicated declaration. Thus, the declaration.

int *p(int 1);

Indicates a function that accepts an integer argument, and returns a pointer to an integer. On the other hand, the declaration:

int (*p) (int a);

Indicates a pointer to a function that accepts an integer argument and returns an integer. In this last declaration, the first pair of parentheses is used for nesting, and the second pair is used to indicate a function. The interpretation of more complex declaration can be increasingly troublesome.

For example, consider the declaration.

int* (*p) (int (*a)[]);

In this declaration, (*p) (….) indicates a pointer to a function. Hence, int *(*p) (….) indicates a pointer to a function that returns a pointer to an integer. Within the last pair of parentheses (the function's argument specification). (*a) [] indicates a pointer to an array. Therefore, int (*a) [] represents a pointer to an array of integers.

Putting the pieces together, (*p) (int (*a) []) represents a pointer to a function whose argument is a pointer to an array of integers. And finally, the entire declaration.

int *(*p) (int (*a) []);

Represents a pointer to a function that accepts a pointer to an array of integers as an argument, and returns a pointer to an integer. Remember that a left parentheses immediately following an identifier name indicates that the identifier represents a function. Similarly, a left square bracket immediately following an identifier name indicates that the identifier represents an array. Parentheses that identify functions and square brackets that identify arrays have a higher precedence than the unary indirection operator, Therefore, additional parentheses are required when declaring a pointer to a function or a pointer to an array.

6.12. DO'S AND DON'TS

- **Do's:**
  - The & sign is used to find out the address of a particular variable in the memory.
  - The * sign is used to find the value at address and indicates a pointer variable.
  - The address of a variable is always a whole number.

  - Printing the value of *(& i) is same printing the value of i.
- **Don'ts:**
  - When you are using an array of pointers to strings you cannot initialize the strings from the keyboard, you can initialize only at the time of declaration.

In pointer arithmetic you cannot perform the operations of multiplication, division. In the beginning of this session you had been briefed about the basics of pointers and its declaration. The different types of pointer variations were then dealt which included the pointer declaration, arithmetic, and comparison. Then two important types of dynamic memory allocation were learnt. The chemistry between pointers and arrays was dealt with. Then assigning a pointer to another pointer was discussed. The array connection with pointers and some extras on pointer declaration was observed.

Going Over It Again:

Fill in the blanks:

1. To find the address of particular variable in the memory the ____________ sign is used.
2. To find the value at address the ______________sign is used.
3. There are ________ methods of dynamic memory allocation.
4. The address of a variable is always a ___________number.

State True or False:

1. In pointer arithmetic the multiplication operation can be performed.
2. The calloc() and malloc() are standard library functions.
3. A pointer variable can store the address of another pointer variable.
4. Printing the value of *(&i) is same as printing the value of i.
5. Pointer comparison between two variables can be done when both the variables do not point to the object of same data type.

One Line Answers:

1. What are the three different pointer variations.
2. What is the difference between calloc() and malloc().
3. What is meant by address of a variable.

CHAPTER 7

Strings

Contents

7.1. INTRODUCTION TO STRINGS

This session is specially focused to attract those people who detest even the first letter of the word mathematics. C has the innate ability to envelop people of various academic backgrounds within its fold. That's what makes C such a widely accepted and appealing language.

In the sessions that you have encompassed till now you had been dealing with only numbers. It was a plethora of numbers everywhere, in arrays, in functions, in pointers you name it and you had it.

Well take a break from numbers and strengthen your potential in English. This doesn't mean you will be writing books in this session. It is just that you will discover a means to store and manipulate alphabets using a few commands.

To recapitulate, in arrays apart from storing integers in a contiguous manner you were also able to extend the above theory to characters and that the first character occupied the 0th position and so on. Unless your concept of arrays are strong any attempt on strings would turn out to be unproductive and futile. You can actually add, compare, and copy strings, to name just a few of the functions performed by the strings. Not squandering anymore of your precious time the definition and description of strings is given below.

7.2. STRINGS

All through your ordeal with C you had been collecting, storing, and displaying numbers, numbers, and only numbers. Only for a brief period of time were you involved in dealing with characters. It's time now to relive that situation. In the brief period that you were introduced to storing characters, it was in arrays. If you remember you were able to store an array of characters which was otherwise called a string. Now it is the same old string that will be the talk of this session and will be dealt with meticulously.

Various programming languages use these character arrays or strings to manipulate text such as words and sentences. To put it across in a definition a string is a one dimensional array of characters and is terminated by a null('\0') and each character occupies only one byte in the memory. Everything said above must be quite comprehensible except the null (\0) character.

It is actually the string terminator or in simple words it is the stop sign for the compiler. Whenever the compiler comes across this null character it is informed that there are no more characters that have to be taken care of and that the compiler should terminate its duties from the string. The terminating null character is essential because it is the only way the functions that work with a string can know where the string ends.

The declaration of a string can be done in the following manner. **char str[]="FUHRER";** It is not necessary that every time you declare an array the null (\0) has to be specified at the end of the string. It is the advantage of C that by default it inserts the null character at the end of the string. The memory considers "\0" to be one character and not as two individual entities and also that "\0" and 0 are not the same.

The following program will dispel any doubts prevalent about the basics of strings.

```
#include<stdio.h>
#include<conio.h>
#include<string.h>
void main()
{
char str[]="bond";
int i;
clrscr();
```

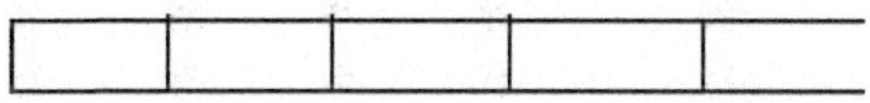

```
for(i=0;str[i]!='\0';i++)
{
printf("%c",str[i]);
}
getch();
}
```

The above program displays the string that is initialized to array str[]. In this program you will encounter a few new things the first of which being the one in line number 2. This is a standard library function which enables the operation of two new functions which are clrscr(); (line number 7) and the getch() (line number 13).

The clrscr() is a function for clearing the screen at the time of displaying the output. And the getch() is used so that the user has to enter some value.

In line number 5, as you can see, the character array is initialized to the string in the quotations. The initialized string is entered into an array using the for loop in line number 9. Apart from initializing the i value to 0 the condition in the for loop is set such that the value of i is not equal to 0, i.e., to say the string will be entered into the loop until there are no more characters to be entered and i encounter the null character.

To print the string in the array the printf statement is given which is shown in line number 11. You will also notice here that the format specifier is % C because character array is being entered.

7.3. INTERNAL REPRESENTATION OF STRINGS

After your initial stint with strings and having written your first program using strings, it would be reasonable to say that you must be aware of the internal representation of the strings. In this section you will get an overview of how these strings are stored in the memory. The strings representation is no different from that of the integer arrays in the sense that all the characters that constitute the string are stored in contiguous memory locations. That is to say the first character will be stored in the 0th position and the second in the 1st and so on.

The last character as you know is the null character. You will now see how the string is stored in the memory.

B O N D \0 1234 1235 1236 1237 1238

As you can see the string bond is stored in a sequential manner and each character occupies one byte each but the point to observe here is that the string is terminated with a null character.

Another word about the length of the string is that if the length of a string is predefined, i.e., the number of spaces in the memory to be reserved for the particular string, then the null character is placed immediately after the last character and the rest of the spaces reserved are left empty. E.g., if the string is declared as char str[10]= “bond”; The representation of the above string would be in the following fashion.

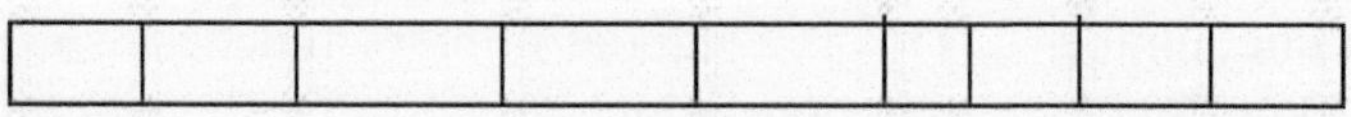

B O N D \0. As you can see after the null character the rest of the spaces are lying empty and this is not a healthy sign for the programmer.

7.4. MORE ON STRINGS

Now that you are informed about strings and their terminator and how these characters are represented in the memory you can march into some more details about the strings which include the variations in the format specifiers and the usage of multiword strings. Well don't be intimidated by this technical jargon and take a dislike towards strings but read on about the various aspects of strings.

The variations that you were informed are that there can be a change in the format specifiers, i.e., to say in the first program you were using %c which is perfectly valid when the string was initialized at the declaration point but if the string has to be accepted from the user at the time of display then a problem arises. To counter act the situation 'C' advises a change in the format specifier from %C to %S.

Take a look below and things will be crystal clear.

```
#include<stdio.h>
#include<conio.h>
void main()
{
char str[20];
clrscr();
printf("Enter name");
scanf("%s", str);
printf("The name entered is %s", str);
getch();
}
```

From the above program you can infer that the strings size is declared to 20 and the string is being requested from the user which is accepted using the format specifier %s in scanf(). If you still can't comprehend the above details take it as a rule that whenever a string is being accepted from the user a %s should be visible in the scanf().

Once the size is declared to 20 the computer sets aside 20 bytes under that array name and a '\0' is placed after the string is entered from the keyboard. There is just one minor hiccup in the concept explained until now. It is that multiword strings are not acceptable by scanf(), i.e., spaces in between 2 words is not valid for example Sarah Gotfried is acceptable. But C takes care of this obstacle adequately. To achieve this feat 'C' uses the functions gets() and puts(). The gets() is similar to the scanf and puts the printf. It is just that gets() and puts() lend an additional aid to strings.

Take look at how it is used in a program.

```
#include<stdio.h>
#include<conio.h>
#include<string.h>
void main()
{
char name[20];
clrscr();
printf("Enter your name:");
gets(name); puts("Hi");
puts(name);
getch();
}
```

The output of the above program will be as follows:

Enter your name: prince william

Hi prince william

One thing to be observed in the above program is that the puts() can display only one string at a time. That's the reason for the appearance of two puts () functions. String Functions You felt manipulations of numbers were easy. Adding, comparing was all child's play to you. Bet you will have a hard time trying the same things out with strings.

The reason is that there are absolutely no operators in C which can be used on strings. You cannot add two strings by stating.

```
str3=str1+str2;
```

This is Blasphemous. Well as usual C provides an alternative which turns out to be an effective one at that. The C standard library provides you with a whole range of functions which specialize in string manipulation (see appendix – B). There are numerous string functions which perform all kinds of odd jobs on strings. To invoke these functions you have to make a special declaration similar to the #include <stdio.h>. But the variation is that it will read as follows:

#include<string.h>.

Since you are running against time and it is practically impossible to explain each one of the functions you will be dealing with 4 major leaders of the cult.

strlen();

strcpy ();

strcat ();

strcmp();

You shall now deal with each one of the big boys individually and try to comprehend their duties.

strlen ()

The strlen() can be used to calculate the length of the string. To find the length of the string all you have to do is pass the string as a parameter within the parentheses and the strlen computes the length and returns it which can be captured in a suitable variables of yours. Note

The null byte is not counted during string length calculation:

```
#include<stdio.h>
#include<conio.h>
#include<string.h>
main()
{
char arr[]="martin";
int len1,len2;
clrscr();
len1=strlen(arr);
len2=strlen("short");
printf("\n%slength=%d",arr,len1); printf("\
n%slength=%d","short",len2);
getch();
}
```

In the above program the first string whose length has to be found is initialized using an array and the second stringis mentioned in the parentheses of the function itself.

strcpy()

The strcpy () function of the C allows you to copy the contents of one string into another. The strcpy within the parentheses takes two parameters the first one for the destination and the second one for the source.

strcpy (destination, source);

The rule to be followed here is that the destination strings must always be a variable or in other words it must be empty. Rewriting on an already existing string is illegal. Once the function is in process it continues copying the character in the source string to the target until it doesn't encounter the end of the source string or in other words the null character (\0).

It is the programmers responsibility that the string doesn't exceed its dimension.

```
#include<stdio.h>
#include<conio.h>
void main()
{
char sour[]="chao";
char dest[10];
clrscr();
strcpy(dest,sour);
printf("\n destination is %s",dest);
printf("\n source is %s", sour);
getch();
}
```

Thus the function of strcpy can be incorporated into a 'C' program in the above depicted manner and the code would be as follows. destination is chao source is chao If you can notice the destination array is uninitialized and empty with the size declared so that it can accommodate the source string which is initialized while declaring. The destination and source string are mentioned within the parentheses of the function with the destination preceding the source.

strcat()

If you were worried that you couldn't add two strings using a "+" operator here is a simpler, more effective way to deal with addition of 2 strings. This can be done using strcat() for example, if you want to concatenate (or add)

"Birds" and "Sing." On using strcat () the final result will be Birds Sing. Just take a look at how the strcat puts its act together. Even in the strcat two parameters have to be accommodated. The first one is the destination to which source string is to be added. The destination is string should have enough space to store the source string that results from the concatenation.

```
#include<stdio.h>
#include<conio.h>
void main()
{
char sour[]="sing";
char dest[15]= "birds";
clrscr(); strcat(dest,sour);
printf("\n source is %s", sour);
printf("\nconcatenated string is%s", dest);
getch();
}
```

The output of the above program would be Source is sing Concatenated string = birds sing

strcmp()

This function is basically used to compare two strings for their equality to see whether they are identical or not. The two strings to be compared are done so until there is a mismatch or the end of any one of the strings is reached, which ever occurs first. If the two strings are identical strcmp() returns a value zero. If they are not equal, it returns the numeric difference between the ASCII values if the non matching characters ASCII values are numbers allocated to alphabets by the computer because it understands only numeric languages.

The program designed below is a representation of strcmp().

```
#include<stdio.h>
#include<conio.h>
void main()
{
char s1[]="mad";
char s2[]="dad";
```

```
int a,b;
clrscr();
a=strcmp(s1,"mad");
b=strcmp(s2,s1);
printf("\n%d\n%d",a,b);
getch();
}
```

The output of the above program would be 0 –9 0 is for the first comparison because both the parameters were evaluated to be similar. –9 is for the second comparison because the difference between m and d and the ASCII value of m is 77 & that of d it 68 and their difference would be 9. If b=strcmp(s1,s2) the output will be 0 and 9. As you might have noticed even in the strcmp() two parameters have to be mentioned, they are the ones that have to be compared with each other.

7.5. PASSING STRINGS TO FUNCTIONS

Write a few functions now, that operate on strings. The first that you shall write is a function which will convert a given word to upper case. Since it is sufficient if the function achieves the conversion and need not really return any thing at all, you can make it a void function.

See the function declaration below:

```
#include<stdio.h>
#include<conio.h>
void main()
{
int i=0;
char str[20];
clrscr();
scanf("%[^\n]",str);
while(str[i] !=0)
{
if(str[i]>='a' && str[i]<='z')
str[i]=str[i]-32;
```

```
i++;
}
printf("%s",str);
getch();
}
```

In the above program the function itself does very little. Starting from the 0th element it scans the string character by character, and whenever it encounters a lower case letter, converts it to upper case. See how the formal parameter is declared. The declaration does not specify the size of the array. When an array is a formal parameter do not specify the size.

For one thing, you are not trying to allocate memory. Memory allocation for the string has been done elsewhere. For another, the caller can pass differently sized arrays. So, it does not make sense to supply the size when an array is a formal parameter to the function.

7.6. TWO-DIMENSIONAL ARRAY OF CHARACTERS

The strings that you have been dealing with until now were all one dimensional arrays and seemed pretty simple and elementary. But what is the effect of two dimensional arrays on the strings. Strings can handle two dimensional array of characters effectively and efficiently. The program given below is a simple example that involves a two dimensional array of characters which includes some new details that will be discussed after the program.

```
#include<stdio.h>
#include<conio.h>
#include<string.h>
void main()
{
char codelist[6][10]=
{
"alpha",
"bravo",
"charlie",
"delta",
```

```
"echo",
"zulu"
};
int i,flag,a;
char code[10];
clrscr();
printf("Enter your password");
scanf("%s",code);
flag=0;
for(i=0;i<=5;i++)
{
a = strcmp(&codelist[i][0],code);
if(a==0)
{
printf("Access granted");
flag=1;
break;
}
}
if(flag==0)
{
printf("Access denied");
printf("you are a spy");
}
getch();
}
```

The above program is to check the user specified password with the list specified at the initialization of the string and based on the string entered either of the printf statements are executed. In the program the initialization carries a lot of importance and should be comprehended before proceeding any further. In the initialization in line 6 the subscripts declared, i.e., 6 and 10 are important.

The subscript 6 specifies the number of names in the array and the 10 specifies the length of each of these names. The names are then declared within a pair of braces. The string comparision statement in line 22 is done between the two strings. The code list along with the subscripts is compared with the user specified word using the for loop. The row subscript is initialized to i and each time the i is incremented which causes the next name to take the place and be compared with the user name. This is done for all the names until a right match is found. If a right match is found the strcmp assigns the value 0 to the variable a.

The flag is used to keep a record of whether the control did reach inside the if or not. If the value of a becomes 0 the flag is re-initialized to 1, i.e., a perfect match is found. If the value of a is not 0 the flag ignores the re-initialization and carries on to the next if statement in line 30.

7.7. ARRAY OF POINTERS

The array of pointers is a replacement for the two dimensional array of characters. The reason being that in the two dimensional the array length is fixed once it is declared and if a string is much smaller than what is specified the rest of the space is empty and wasted. Using the array of pointers can erase these side effects.

Thus one reason to store strings in an array of pointers is to make more efficient use of the available memory. Another reason is that using the pointers can also help you to manipulate the strings just like the library functions. Below is a program that interchanges the two names that are specified in the printf statements.

```
#include<stdio.h>
#include<conio.h>
void main()
{
char *str[]={"bill", "croft", "jude", "nancy", "robert,", "peter"};
char *temp;
clrscr();
printf("unchanged=%s %s",str[2],str[3]);
temp=str[2];
str[2]=str[3];
```

```
str[3]=temp;
printf("\n changed=%s %s",str[2],str[3]);
getch();
}
```

The output of the above program would be as follows:

unchanged=jude nancy changed=nancy jude

The above program is an example that interchanges the names in two locations of the array using the addresses of the names. The names are initialized in the array and the names to be exchanged are specified in the logic of the program. The names are interchanged using a temporary variable called temp and the names that are interchanged are printed using the printf statements.

7.8. DO'S AND DON'TS

- **Do's:**
  - The null character should be enclosed within a pair of single quotes. ('\0')
  - The standard library functions should be terminated with a semicolon.

  E.g., strcpy();
  - The %s should be used when the string is to be accepted from the user.
  - The clrscr() should be declared after the variable declarations are done.
- **Don'ts:**
  - The length of the string should not exceed the dimension of the character array.
  - The scanf() is not capable of receiving multiword strings unless altered with gets()
  - And the format specifier "%[^\n]"
  - In strcpy() the destination has to be a variable because overwriting of an already existing string is not possible.

7.9. SUMMARY

In this session you had a detailed look at strings and their characteristics along with an idea as how they are represented in the memory. Then the important standard string functions which are the strlen(), strcpy(), strcat() and the strcmp() were introduced and explained with examples. You then learnt how to implement strings into functions, pointers, and arrays. The session concluded with a regular dose of Do's and Don'ts.

Going Over it Again:

Fill in the blanks:

1. The ________________ is placed immediately after the last character.
2. The addition of two strings is possible using ________ function.
3. If two strings are identical the strcmp() returns _________.
4. The standard library functions should be terminated with a _________.
5. The ______ format specifier must be used if strings are to be accepted from the user.

State True or False:

1. The null is not counted during string calculation.
2. Rewriting on an already existing string is valid.
3. The clrscr() should be declared after the variable declarations are done.
4. The format specifier "%[^\n]" is capable of receiving multiword strings.
5. If the two strings in strcmp() are not identical zero is returned.

One Line Answers:

1. What is the use of the function strcpy()?
2. What is a string?
3. What is the function of the null character?

CHAPTER 8

Structures

Contents

8.1. INTRODUCTION TO STRUCTURES

The basics are now surpassed milestones, conquered forts but the best is yet to come and the final whistle yet to be blown and miles to go before you bid adieu to C. The concepts no more remain to be the dark dirty clouds but they clear the horizons of the dust and dirt to build a bridge between the seen and the unexplored the rigid and the intangible. After having grappling with the nuances of C in the earlier sessions its time now to meet the street-smart types.

The earlier concepts are useful for small time programming skills but you are now presented with a concept that can be applied in day to day life that too effectively and impeccably. Imagine storing the personal and official details of the staff of an entire organization in C program. By conventional means it would take a few hundred lines of codes with a humungous amount of variables and keywords.

These are just a few of the hiccups that will be encountered. But can this redundancy be avoided or if not be reduced to a minimal extent? Using structures it can. Judging from the name, one may formulate structures to be some kind of a illustration or a figure of some sorts. Well as some learned person once said What's in a name? A C structure in no way resembles a figure or can be remotely compared to an illustration. In comparison the structures are like an allrounder who excels in any of the 0, 45 and center positions in a game of basketball. The versatility it offers is due to the fact that the structures can encompass all three data types viz. Int, char and float. Earlier you had to declare the variables separately and access them individually but now you can include them into a common roof called structures and access each one of the data types using the subscript of structures. But this is not what it is famous for.

8.2. ELEMENTARY STRUCTURES

After getting just a brief idea of structures it is time to get into the definition of structures. A structure is just another data type of C. But the specialty is it encompasses the rest of the data types, i.e., to say the data types, integer, Character, Float can be declared within this data type and this can be used in the rest of the program. Say you want to store the name, social security number and salary of an employee.

You take three different variables and write a program and there ends the story. But if the above process has to be applied for 75 employees then things would turnout to be pretty tedious especially when you realize that apart from these details you also want to store particulars like his address, the telephone number, license number and so on.

These things can get tedious even with arrays because that many arrays have to be declared and apart from those a battery of for loops have to be declared and the program would go haywire and the number of lines would shoot up beyond expectations and lastly just imagine the error finding process. You would probably spend the rest of your programming life searching for an error. Whew! This is where structures does the superman act.

By declaring the three variables in a structure these variables can be accessed any number of times by just using the subscript of the structure. The Pointer, Arrays, and other Structures can also be inducted as elements within a defined structure. The individual structure elements that is the int, char declared inside a structure are referred to as members of that particular structure. The structure once declared can be accessed and processed within a program.

Apart from this, the structures also spread its tentacles to other aspects of C and are closely associated with the functions, arrays, and pointers. More details will be splashed out in the later parts of this session and you will appreciate the structures once you have a detailed outlook at all those concepts.

8.3. DECLARING AND ACCESSING A STRUCTURE

After having an insight about the advantages and the definition of structure you shall now learn how to declare a structure. As talked of earlier that structure is a data type and like the rest of the data types it is also a keyword and it is written as "struct." This has to be allotted a name referred to as "tag" or simply structure name and below it the different members are mentioned.

These members are nothing but variables with their data types mentioned. The general format is described below:

```
struct tag
{
datatype variable name;
datatype variable name;
};
```

An example is given below:

```
struct employee
{
int eno;
char ename;
float esal;
};
```

From the above, e.g., You can see that the key word struct is mandatory followed by the structure name and it opens braces for the members. The structure members here are the eno, ename, and esal and each of them are terminated with a semi colon and the closing braces for the structure is also terminated with a semicolon. Initializing the members Once the new structure data type has been declared, variables as per the programmers request can be defined of that type For example the structure variables e1,e2,e3 can be declared of the data type struct employee as depicted below:

```
struct employee e1,e2,e3;
```

Now the question arises where do you declare the above statement, this can be done in the following different ways after the closing braces of the structures.

```
};
/* closing brace*/
struct employee e1,e2,e3;
OR
} e1,e2,e3;
```

Once the declaring has been done you need to know if initializing can be done while declaring and the answer is positive. The format must be familiar to you, as it is similar to the one used in arrays. Take a look below at the format:

```
struct employee
{
char ename[10];
float esal;
int eno;
};
struct employee e1 = {" Johnny", 500.00, 101};
```

struct employee e2 = {" Davis", 1000.00,102};

If you are not happy with this type of initializing the other type is to request the user with the help of the scanf(). This type will be dealt with later. Accessing members Now that you have declared and initialized the structure variable it's time to check out how to access the variables so that they can be used in the program (Figure 8.1).

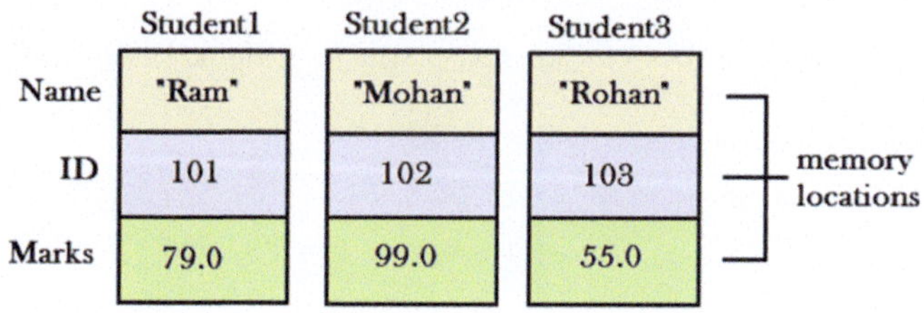

Figure 8.1. Declaring and accessing a structure.

You used a subscript for accessing elements in the array. Here you use a dot(.) to access the data. Say you want the salary of the second employee, then it can be written in the following way. e2.esal The e2 is called the structure variable and esal the element.

A dot must exist between the structure variable and the structure member.

8.4. INTERNAL REPRESENTATION OF THE STRUCTURE

Since so much goes on while declaring, initializing, and accessing a structure where do all the variables and values actually get stored in the memory? All elements of a structure regardless of the number or type are stored in contiguous memory locations and the number of bytes assigned to the data types are the same as before. The internal representation of the details of the first employee, "Johnny" with a salary of 500.00, employee ID of 101, and a few additional numerical values, stored in contiguous memory locations might look like this:

Memory Layout:

Variable Value Memory-Address

E 'E' 0x1000

Name "Johnny" 0x1001

Salary 500.00 0x1008

Employee ID 101 0x100C

Additional 1111 0x1010

Additional 1112 0x1014

Additional 1116 0x1018

A simple program using structure:

```
/* program that accepts values and displays it back */ #include<stdio.h>
void main()
{
struct emp
{
char ename[15];
float esal;
int eno;
};
struct emp e1,e2,e3;
printf("Enter name,salaries and identity number of employees\n");
scanf("%s %f %d",&e1.ename,&e1.esal,&e1.eno);
scanf("%s %f %d",&e2.ename,&e2.esal,&e2.eno);
scanf("%s%f %d",&e3.ename,&e3.esal,&e3.eno); printf("You have entered the following data:");
printf("%s %f %d",e1.ename,e1.esal,e1.eno);
printf("%s %f %d",e2.ename,e2.esal,e2.eno);
printf("%s %f %d",e3.ename,e3.esal,e3.eno);
}
```

In the above program you can see that the structure members are declared inside the structure and the structure variables, i.e., e1, e2, e3 are declared outside the structure using the key word struct and the structure name The values for the structure members are requested from the user and they are accepted using the scanf.

The values are printed back by using the structure variable and the structure member with a dot(.) in between them.

8.5. ARRAY OF STRUCTURES

In the above program you have acclimatized yourself to the various contents in a C program using structures. The above program was perfect, since it received 3 values and displayed them back, but if the number of values was increased to 100 then you might have used 100 structure variables from b1,b2,.......b100 but As magnanimous as C is it always provides an alternative for tedious issues.

The structures in these kind of emergencies request the arrays to act immediately. That is to say the structure variables can be declared as an array and large amount of variables can be used efficiently. To declare an array of structures the process is similar to arrays. Before the square brackets 3 things precede it.

The keyword struct, the structure name and the array name. Thus, the employee array can be declared as below.};

struct employee e[100];

You are now presented with a sample program that will cover all the aspects required to be comprehended in structures using arrays.

```
#include<stdio.h>
struct emp
{
char ename[15];
int esal;
int eno;
};
struct emp e[3];
void main()
{
int i;
for(i=0;i<=2;i++)
{
printf("\n Enter name,salary and idno");
scanf("%s %d %d",&e[i].ename,&e[i].esal,&e[i].eno);
}
for(i=0;i<=2;i++)
```

```
printf("\n %s\n%d\n%d",e[i].ename,e[i].esal,e[i].eno);
}
```

The above simple program accepts names, salaries, and id no of 15 employees and displays it back. As you can see the program accepts 15 names from the user and displays it back using a for loop with the subscript variable I which has to be declared as an int. You can see that the structure has been declared externally before the main() function, so that the elements are accessible to all parts of the program. Once the array of structure is declared, i.e., by giving the statement struct emp e[15], space in the memory is reserved for 15 structure types.

8.6. PASSING STRUCTURE INTO FUNCTIONS

Now that you have had enough knowledge about using arrays in structures its time to knock the door of functions and try and analyze how an entire structure can be passed into a function. Before embarking on that one minor detail what you should be aware of is that individual elements of the structure also can be passed to a function but the only shortcoming in that is if there are many elements then passing those elements to a function would turn out to be a stupendous affair and it is better to refrain from such acts.

Hence the areaof concern for you would be to pass an entire structure to a function. The modus operandi would be just the same and does not differ in any aspect. The one thing to be noted here is that the initialization is done at the time of declaration, i.e., n static mode.

```
#include<stdio.h>
struct emp
{
char ename[10];
int eno;
float esal;
};
void main()
{
struct emp e1={"cooper", 104,6000.00};
pass(e1);
}
```

```
pass(struct emp e)
{
printf("%s\n%d\n%f",e.ename,e.eno,e.esal);
}
```

The output of the above program would be as follows:

cooper 104 6000.00.

In the above program the function used is pass(); and the whole structure is passed using the variable e1 and it is printed in the function.

8.7. POINTERS IN STRUCTURES

Having learnt about functions and arrays it's not fair to leave pointers behind. Since structure is also a data type like the int char, etc. You can have a pointer pointing to a struct. Such kinds of pointers are termed as structure pointers, though there is a difference while accessing these pointer variables. To access the other variables you used a dot (.) but this is not possible in a pointer but instead of a dot (.) you can use an arrow. (->) Since you don't have a particular key for the arrow you use a hyphen (-) and a greater than (>) symbol and that should suffice. The program below uses the above operator (–>) to access the elements and print them. Therefore, things will be pretty comprehendible once you go through the program carefully.

```
#include<stdio.h>
void main()
{
struct emp
{
char ename[10];
int eno;
float esal;
};
struct emp e1={"suzzane",116,7500.00};
struct emp*point; point=&e1;
printf("%s %d %f",e1.ename,e1.eno,e1.esal);
printf("%s %d %f", point->ename,point->eno,point->esal);
```

```
}
```

The first printf statement prints as usual but the second one deserves a close observation. The pointer "point" uses the arrow instead of a dot to access the elements in the variable name and so on. The representation of the above arrangement of variables in the memory is shown in Figure 8.2.

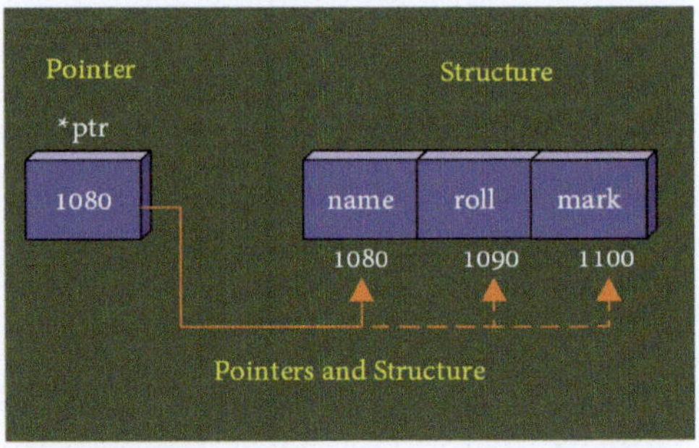

Figure 8.2. Pointer and structure.

8.8. NESTED STRUCTURES

You were earlier introduced to nested control structures like nested if else and nested for, etc. Now it is time to take a look at the nested structures and how they can be created. The following program provides an insight into the intricacies of nested structures.

```
#include<stdio.h>
void main()
{
struct directory
{
char ph[10];
char city[20];
};
struct emp
{
char name[20];
struct directory d;
};
```

```
static struct emp e={"bobby","876876","illinois"};
printf("name=%s\n",e.name);
printf("phone=%s\n",e.d.ph);
printf("city=%s",e.d.city);
}
```

Here you will notice that to access the element of a structure that are enclosed within another structure the dot operated is used twice.

Nesting cannot be restricted to only 2 structures and each of them can be accessed by that many dots. In the above program you can see that a variable d is declared in the nested structure that corresponds to the first structure and using this variable the elements declared in the first structure can be accessed. While printing the elements of both the structures, both the variables e and d are used along with the member name each of them separated with a dot(.)

8.9. THE UNIONS

A union is yet another data type in C, which allows you to overlay more than one variable in the same memory area. Usually the storage procedure is that every variable is stored in separate memory locations and each one of them has a unique address. Often you discover that the variables that you use in the program are used only in a small part of the source.

Let's say that you require a string of length 50 bytes, by name files in the first fifty lines of your source program and assume further that you need another string variable of length 100 bytes with the name display only in the later part of the program. You may now realize that it is not necessary to declare two separate strings which will consume 150 bytes.

Since these variables are not needed simultaneously, it will be highly convenient if both the strings share the same space. A Union does that. There is a striking resemblance between the unions and the structures in the way they are declared, the way the members are accessed and so on. The general format of a union declaration is shown below:

```
union tag
{
member1;
member2
```

```
}
union variable;
```

As you can see a union declaration starts with the key word union, followed by the tag, this is similar to the structures and can bear any name. In between the open and close braces are present the members of the union The amount of memory required to store a structure is the sum of sizes of all the members. On the other hand in the case of unions the amount of memory required is the same as that required for its largest member. The members of a union are accessed using the dot (.) operator just like the structure members are accessed.

8.10. ENUMERATED DATA TYPES

All this while you were using data types such as int, char, etc., that were defined by Ritchie. It's time you turned a bit creative and implemented your own data types in the program. Impossible one may think But with enum it is possible. The enum gives you the opportunity to invent your own data type and define the variables that it can take. You might ask why would anyone want do such a thing when readymade stuff is available.

The advantage it can have is that it can make the program decent looking and readable and more than one programmer will be able to use it. A note about declaring predefined values. In a manner that int has a range of values from –32768 to +32768 and any value within it is recognized by int in a similar way once you define a data type you can specify the values that it can accept.

Only the values mentioned by you will be accepted when the data type is used. Consider you are creating a data type called blood group and you decide to name it as bloodgrp and you assign it 4 values A, B, AB, & O. Then the declaration can be done in the following way:

```
enum bloodgrp {a, b, ab, o};
enum bloodgrp person1, person2;
```

If you notice in the above declaration, you will find a great amount of similarity with the declaration of structures. The first part declares the data type and specifies its possible values. These values are called enumerators and the keyword used here is "enum." The second part declares variables of this data type. Now values can be assigned to these variables in the following manner:

person1 = ab;

person2 = o;

The compiler treats the enumerators as intergers internally. Thus, the first value declared will be assigned a value 0 and the second 1 and so on. Therefore, in the above example the value of enum bloodgrp will contain the following values:

a = 0 b = 1 ab = 2 o = 3

Any other value other than a, b, ab, and o will not be accepted and would cause an error. Enumerated data types are usually used to clarify the operation of a program and it makes listing easier.

8.11. THE TYPEDEF STATEMENT

This is one more method in C which comes handy in situations where clarification of source code of a C program is required. This can be considered as a nickname for a data type that has a long name. The typedef is useful in the sense that it helps us to assign short readable names to data types. For example, the data type unsigned long int can be renamed as nick. It can be any word of the user's choice and it is preferable that the rechristened name be mentioned in capitals. The following example shows the way of declaring a typedef statement. The keyword here is typedef which is followed by the original data type name which is followed by the new user defined name in capitals.

typedef unsigned long int NICK;

Once this is done the new name NICK can be used for declaring the data type of a particular variable Example:

NICK variable1, variable2;

Thus the usage of typedef provides a short and meaningful way to call a data type.

8.12. DO'S AND DON'TS

As usual the general features and the regulations of game have to be short listed and presented for your quick reference. The do's and don'ts guide you through your endeavor with this session. A few of the norms that are to be followed while utilizing the concepts of this session are given below.

- **Do's:**
  - The structure declaration should be terminated using the

closing braces and a semicolon.

- The tag in structures and unions is not mandatory.
- While accessing members there must be a dot(.) in between the structure variable and the structure member.
- Structure type declaration appears at the top of the source code file before the variables or the functions are declared.

- **Don'ts:**
  - While accessing members in structures using pointers don't use the dot. Instead it is replaced with an arrow.
  - A structure type declaration does not tell the compiler to reserve any space in the memory, it just defines the form of the structure.

8.13. SUMMARY

In this session you had a variety of concepts which were interrelated to each other. You started with the structures and learnt the means of declaring, initializing, and accessing the structures. The relationship with other aspects of C such as arrays, pointers, and functions were dealt effectively. The structures were concluded with the nested structures and this was followed by the unions which bore a close resemblance with structures. Two new concepts were dwelt upon at the end of the session which were the enum's and the typedef statement. The session was finally concluded with the do's and don'ts of this session.

Going Over It Again:

Fill in the blanks:

1. __________________ Statement is used to define any variable in C.
2. __________________ Declaration is used store data for more than one variable in the same space.
3. _____________________ in structures and unions is mandatory.
4. You can create your own data type by using the key word __________________.
5. Structure inside a structure is called __________________.

State True or False:

1. Structure is a data type, which has a key word called struct.
2. We cannot use pointers in a structure.
3. You need to use the arrow (->) to access elements in structures, if you are using pointers.
4. All the elements of a given structure are stored in contiguous memory locations.
5. Initializing a structure is not required.

One Line Answers:

1. How do you pass functions to any structure?
2. How do you declare and access a structure?
3. What is a union?

CHAPTER 9

Data Structures

Contents

9.1. INTRODUCTION

After learning about data structures part one it's time to meet the twin brother of the data structures. The second saga of data structures deals with the details of representing a list of elements of a data structure. All through your journey in this session you find that some parts of the session bear striking resemblance to the arrays.

The entire session concentrates on ways of juggling with a list of numbers. The concepts to be narrowed down here are the fundamental building blocks for programming a list of numbers in any language. You will be startled to know that this logic holds water even for most of the high level languages. You may feel that these concepts could have been brought to light at an earlier stage but to appreciate the effectiveness of this version of the data structures a thorough knowledge of arrays and pointers is always advisable.

9.2. LINKED LISTS

To explain the concepts of linked lists an amalgamated reference of the arrays and pointers has to be made. The reason why linked lists are so important and are given a priority is due to the fact that they result in both the effective and efficient use of computer storage and also computer time. The concept that is going to be dealt with here is similar to the arrays except that in arrays only application side was discussed in detail and internal representation was dealt to a very minimal extent. Here you will be provided with extensive amount of information about internal happenings of the arrays using linked lists as the medium.

A linked lists can be compared with a train. As in a train the different compartments are hooked to each other in the similar way a linked list has a series of elements which are connected to each other. Each element in a list is called a node and it has an address by which it is recognized. The linked lists are of three different types depending on the arrangement of the nodes.

- Singly linked list
- Doubly linked list
- Circular linked list

The singly and doubly linked lists can be clubbed into a group called the linear linked lists in which the elements are arranged in a serial and contiguous fashion. The intricacies of these 2 types of linked lists will be dealt with as the session progresses.

9.3. SINGLY LINKED LISTS

Prior to understanding the specifics of singly linked lists, it is crucial to have a solid understanding of the node, which is a list's fundamental building block.

The fundamental part of a list is the node, as was previously stated. There are two elements to it; the first is referred to as the info and the second as the connection Node.Info Link The info part of the node contains information about the node that is what number is stored in the node or which character is stored in the node.

The link part of the node contains the address of the next node. As informed in the earlier sessions that whenever a value is stored on the memory it is stored at a particular address. As a result, the address of the second node in a singly linked list with four nodes or elements is stored in the link area of the first node, the address of the third node in the link area of the second, and so on (Figure 9.1).

You may wonder what the link area of the 4th node would contain. The 4th link area contains a null character, which depicts the end of the link. (If you remember a string was also terminated in the same fashion.)

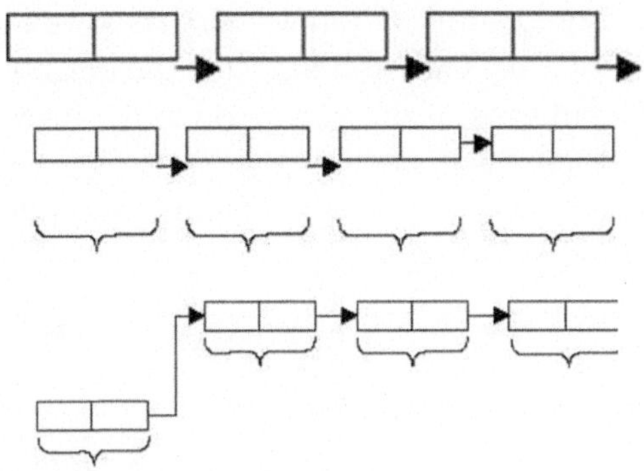

Figure 9.1. Singly linked lists.

Thus the list can be represented as follows:

Info link Info link Info link Info Null A 2010 B 2012 C 2014 D Null 2008 2010 2012 2014

The elements in the linked lists can be traversed using a pointer called head pointer which points to the first element of the list. This head pointer can be used to traverse the elements of the list from left to right and traversal of elements is possible only in this direction.

Random access is illegal, i.e., you cannot access the 2nd or the 3rd element of the list directly. You are aware of the fact that the one that holds the address of another element is called a pointer. Thus, the link can also be called the pointer because it points to the next element in the list.

Now that you have a clear picture about the singly linked lists you will see how the inserting and deleting operations are performed on this linked list. Insertions The insertion operation in the singly linked list can be performed at three different positions in the singly linked list.

- At the beginning of the list.
- At the end of the list.
- In between two nodes.

If the insertion of a new node has to made at the beginning of the list the link area of the new node is assigned the address of the first node. The head pointer is then made to point to the new first element. Since it contains the address of the old first element a link is created between the new node and the rest of the list. A 2010 2008 A 2008 B 2012 A 2014 2010 2012 NEW

An insertion operation can be performed on the middle of the list in between two nodes. For example if a new node has to be inserted in between the 2nd and 3rd nodes in a list then as a first step the head pointer is traversed till the 2nd node. The address of the new node to the inserted is assigned to the link area of the 2nd node and the link area of the new node is assigned the address of the 3rd node. Thus, a link is broken between the 2nd and 3rd node and new node is inserted.

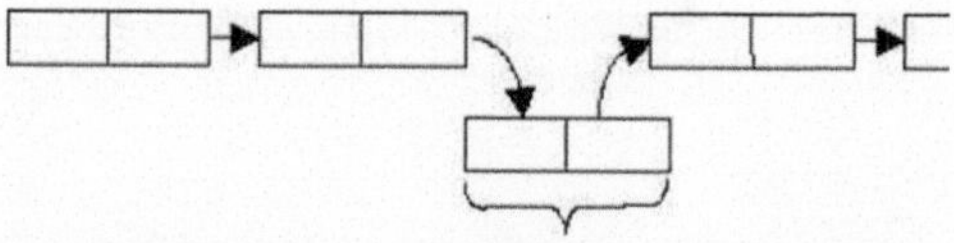

A 2008 B 2016 C 2014 In X 2012 2016

For a node to be inserted at the end of the list the head pointer is traversed till the last node and the link area which contains null is reassigned to hold the address of the new node and the new node is assigned the null character in its link area. The process of insertion precedes a search for the place of insertion. The search involves locating a node after which the new item is to be inserted.

A general algorithm for insertion is as follows:

1. **Algorithm Begin:** If the list is empty or the new node comes before the head node then, Insert the new node as the head node, Else If the new node comes after the last node, then, Insert the new node as the end node, Else Insert the new node in the body of the list. End.
2. **Deletion Operator:** The deletion operation also consists of 3 phases but the operational procedure is quite different to the insertion.

   The three types by which the deletion operation can be performed are:

- Deleting the first node;
- Deleting the last node;
- Deleting between two nodes.

9.3.1. Deleting the First Node

For the deletion of the first node from the list the second node is assigned the head pointer. Once this is done the 2nd node becomes the first node and the previous node is deleted.

9.3.2. Deleting the Last Node

In this the head pointer is traversed to the second last node and the link area is assigned a null. Thus, it becomes the last node of the linked list.

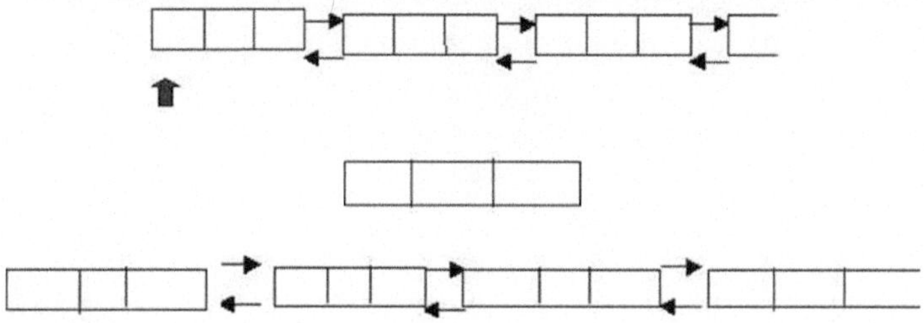

9.3.3. Deleting in Between 2 Nodes

For example if the deletion operation has to be performed on the 3rd node then the head pointer is traversed up to 2nd node and the link area is assigned the address of the 4th node and the 4th element automatically gets deleted.

Algorithm Begin if the list is empty, then, node cannot be deleted, else if node to be deleted is the first node, then, make the head point to the second node, else delete the node from the body of the list. End

9.4. DOUBLY LINKED LISTS

The singly linked list proved to be advantageous but there were more disadvantages than advantages. Using the singly linked list any element could not be accessed directly. If the last element had to be accessed the whole list had to be traversed which was time consuming and cumbersome.

One more flaw was that the traversing of elements was not possible from a right to left direction. These shortcomings can be overcome by using the doubly linked list. This is just a slight modification of the singly linked list. The mode of the doubly linked list has an extra link area on its left side. Thus, it would look like this. Link info Link You have already been apprised that the right link area contains the address of the next element. In a similar way the left link area contains the address of the predecessor node.

A list containing this type of node is called a doubly linked list or a two way chain. Null A &B Null A &B Null A &B Null A &B Thus the left link of the left most node and right link of the right most node will contain a null. In a way similar to the singly linked list even the doubly linked list has a head pointer for traversal from left to right. But in addition, the doubly linked list also has an extra pointer which dons the role of the head pointer and it is used for traversing the list from right to left. The left head pointer points at the first element of the list and right the last element.

Thus pictorially it can be represented as follows: A B C L The insertion and deletion operations can be performed on a doubly linked list with much more efficacy and speed than compared to the singly linked list (Figure 9.2).

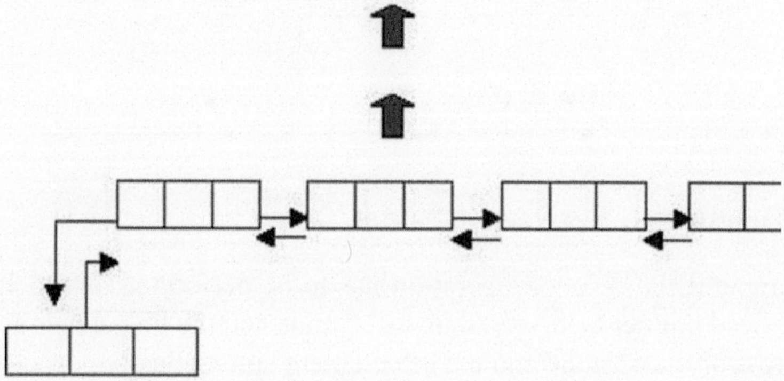

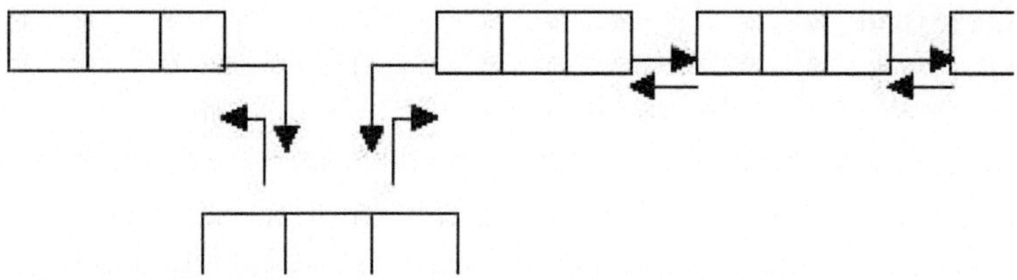

Figure 9.2. Doubly linked lists.

9.4.1. Insertion

Insertion operation in a doubly linked list can be performed at three different locations:

- If list is empty and the first node has to be inserted;
- Beginning of a list; and
- In between two nodes.

Consider the consequence of inserting a node if a list is empty. The insertion in such a case can be performed by assigning the L and R pointers to the same node and the link areas of left and right will contain Null.

9.4.2. Null

A Null L R Now if a node has to be inserted in the beginning of the list or in other words the insertion has to be done to the left of the left most node of the list. In such a case the right link of the new node is assigned the address of the first node and left link is assigned address of new node and the head pointer 'L' is affixed to the new node.

A B C D Null X Finally, if an insertion has to be made in between two nodes it can be done in the following depicted manner.

Null A B C X A general algorithm for inserting a node is given below. Algorithm Obtain a new new node and set its fields. If the list is empty then insert the node in the list update left and right pointers to the list and return If the node is to be inserted at the front of the list then insert the node update the left pointer to the list and return Insert the node in the middle of the list and return.

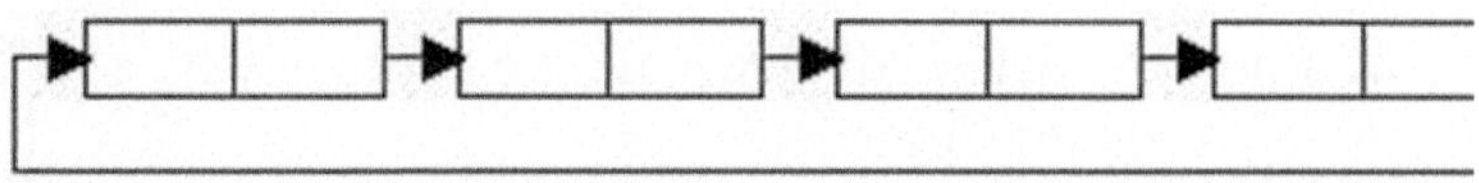

9.4.3. Deletion

You may recollect that the deletion of node in a singly linked list entailed in finding the predecessor of the discarded node and the deletion was done. The search was done by chaining through successive nodes. The search was mandatory and such a search can be quite cumbersome and it could become painstaking if the list was long and number of nodes to be deleted was more. In a doubly linked list no such search is required. Given the address of the node which is to be deleted its successor and predecessor nodes can be known immediately. Similar to the insertion operation the deletion operation also can be performed in the following locations:

- If list is empty;
- At the beginning of the list;
- In between the nodes.

9.5. CIRCULAR LINKED LISTS

The early parts of the session were exclusively concerned with the linked linear lists and its different forms performing variant functions. All the linked lists that you have dealt so far had one thing in common. They were terminated with a null. A slight modulation in the structure of the linked list can now be performed which results in improving the processing the list. The circular linked lists believes that there is no need for the existence of the null and that the integrity of the linked list can be maintained and revamped without the null. This is accomplished by replacing the null in last node with the address of the first node. With the incorporation of the circular linked list a few rules, which held water earlier, are bent. The first of them of being that there is no first node once a circular list is created. The node where the head pointer is made to point in a circular list becomes the starting point for traversing the list. Thus, any node of your choice can be accessed directly for the first time. To examine the effectiveness of the circular list, it's coexistence in both the forms of the linear linked lists is evaluated. Thus, there can exist:

1. **Circular Singly Linked List:** In circular singly linked lists, the null pointer in the last node of a singly linked list is replaced with the address of the first node of the list. By achieving the above feat a circular singly linked list is created and the accessibility of a node is increased. Hence all the nodes can be accessed by merely scanning through the list.

A &B B &C C &D D &A

An added advantage is evident during the deletion operations. For the deletion operation to be performed in singly linked list the predecessor node of the deleted node had to be found. This required an intensive search and traversal process starting from the first node.

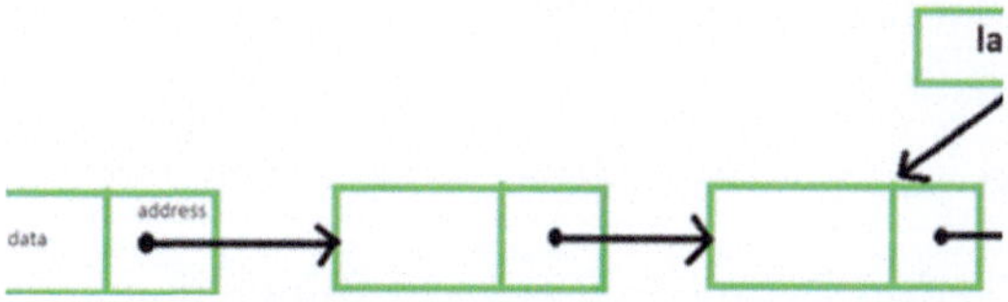

The circular list avoids such a cumbersome process because as mentioned earlier any node can be accessed directly and the list can be traversed from there. A minor drawback is however detected in the circular list. Using the circular list there is high risk of the list ending in an indefinite loop, if proper care is not taken while processing. To avoid complication the end of the list has to be identified. This can be done by placing a special node often referred to as list head in the circular list.

2. **Circular Doubly Linked Lists:** For the doubly linked list to be made a circular list the null present in the right link of the last node of the list is replaced with the address of the first node and similarly the null in the left link of the first node is replaced with the address of last node.

   Thus a circular doubly linked list is created which can be pictured as follows:

   &D A B C D

   For simplification of the insertion and deletion operation a special node called the head node is used. This is similar to the list head in circular singly linked list. By using the head node a certain degree of symmetry is maintained in the structure of the circular linked list.

   The right link of the right most node contains the address of the head node and left link of the head node points to the right most node (Figure 9.3).

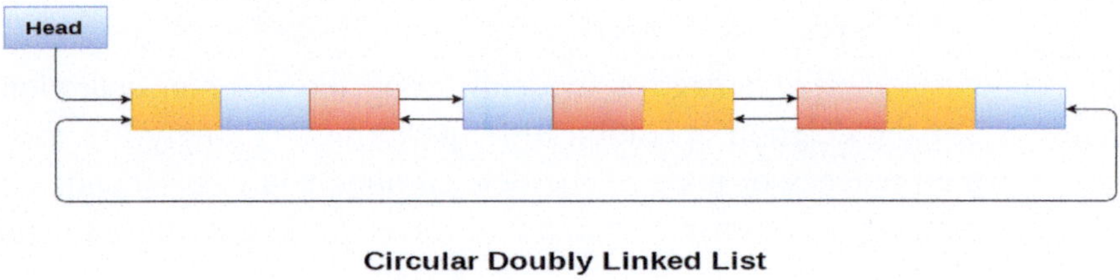

Figure 9.3. Circular doubly linked list.

9.6. STACKS

In the above procedures you experienced a minimal amount of difficulty in creating a list and performing insertions and deletions of the list. Here is a linear data structure, which cannot be termed ineffectual, but is definitely not very popular when a consensus is required and yet remains to be an important data structure concept.

The stack as it is termed is a list of elements placed on top of each other. This can be compared to a pile of plates arranged one above the other. Thus, after the arrangement of the plates you will notice that the first plate finds the bottom most position and last plate to be placed, will acquire the first position. Thus, with reference to the elements when the second element is added to the list it causes the first one to be pushed down the stack and when the third is added the 2nd and 1st are pushed down and so on.

Thus it can be visualized like a cylinder with only the top end open and as the number of elements increases, the size of the cylinder also increases. This process is called insertion in a stack (Figure 9.4). 1 7th 2 6th 6th 3 5th 5th 4 4th 4th 5 3rd 3rd 6 2nd 2nd 7 1st 1st TOP element to be:

H 1 A 2 R 3 R 4 Y 5

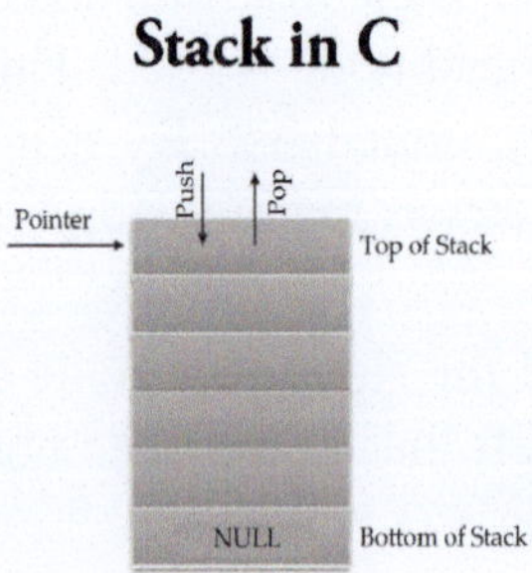

Figure 9.4. Stack in C programming.

The above diagram is a pictorial representation of a seven element stack. A pointer always points to the top most position of the stack which is an indicator of where the insertions have to be performed. Each time an insertion of an element is activated the pointer top is incremented so that it retains its top-most position in the stack. The insertion operation is also called push.

LIFO The expanded version of the lifo(pronounced as leefo) is called the last in first out and lifo mainly deals with the deletion operation of the stack. As the name suggests whenever a deletion operation is to be performed the last element to be inserted into the stack would be first element that will be deleted from the stack for example when a set of tennis balls are to be extracted from its case, the first ball to be removed would be the last one that was placed in the case.

Thus, in the above diagram if the deletion operation has to be performed on the string HARRY the first element to be deleted would be H followed by A and so on. Deletion operation in a stack is also referred to as pop. Example: H A R R Y

9.7. QUEUES

The disadvantages of stacks that were so prominent can be alleviated to some extent using the queues. The queues are particularly helpful in the deletion operation. The queues as the name suggests is a set of elements that are placed one after another, just like people standing in a queue at the reservation counter of a cinema hall (Figure 9.5).

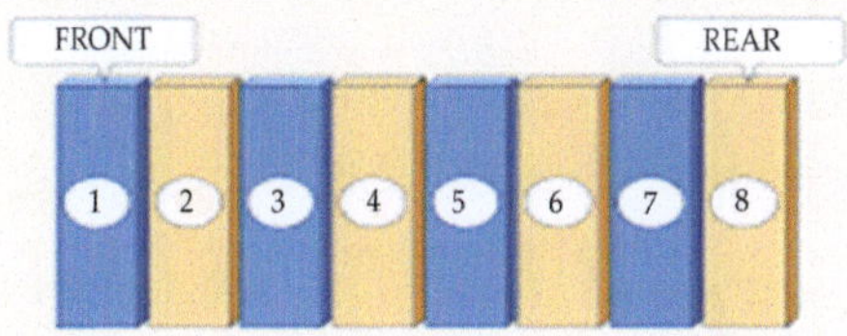

Figure 9.5. Queue in C.

The difference between the stacks and queues is that the first element to be entered will also be the first element to exit the queue which is on a first come first served basis. This kind of representation can also be termed as FIFO. 1st Element to be

Rear Frontal Insertion Deletion FIFO FIFO (pronounced as feefo) when expanded calls itself first in first out.

This is quite in contrast to the LIFO where insertion and deletion could be performed only at one end but in FIFO the insertion is done at one end and the deletion at the other. An apt example would be to consider a queue of cars at a check post and the first car to arrive at the check post would be the first car to be checked and cleared from the post.

Thus, in the FIFO manner each deletion removes the oldest remaining element in the structure. DEQUE A deque otherwise deciphered as a double-ended queue, is an improved version of an ordinary queue. Using the deque the insertions and deletions can be made from either end of the list. That is to say the insertion or deletion can be performed from the front end or the rear end. The process is represented in the following manner.

There are two variations of deque.

1. Input restricted deque; and
2. Output restricted deque.

The input restricted deque allows insertions only at one end whereas an output restricted deque permits deletions from only one end.

9.7.1. Priority Queue

A priority queue is a version of the queue in which you are able to insert elements or remove elements from any position based on some particular priority. Consider an example of a time sharing computer system where many users share the system simultaneously.

In these kinds of systems the resources such as memory must be shared by allocating a short time to one user followed by the next. In some cases based on the intensity of the program a user who is not in a queue may be allotted resources, before his predecessors. Such a queue is called priority queue with priority numbers such as 1,2,3, etc.

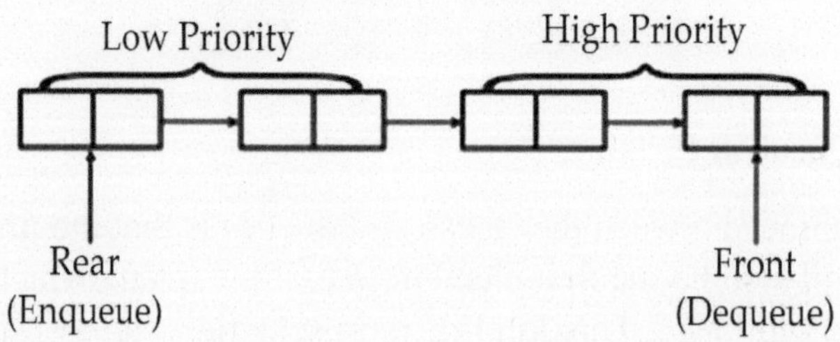

9.8. BINARY TREES

Earlier in this session, you have stumbled upon different means of storing elements and also the various means of representing the elements, their prominent features and also their shortcomings. Presented to you now is yet another concept of representing elements. The binary tree.

Before discussing the binary tree you have to understand what a tree is. A tree with reference to the data structures is similar to a hierarchical representation of an organization. In an organization you have a director right on top with a selected few managers as his lieutenants who have a number of superiors with a union of workers reporting to them. In 6th 5th 4th 3rd 2nd 1st 6th 5th 4th 3rd 2nd 1st Insertion Deletion, Deletion (Figure 9.6).

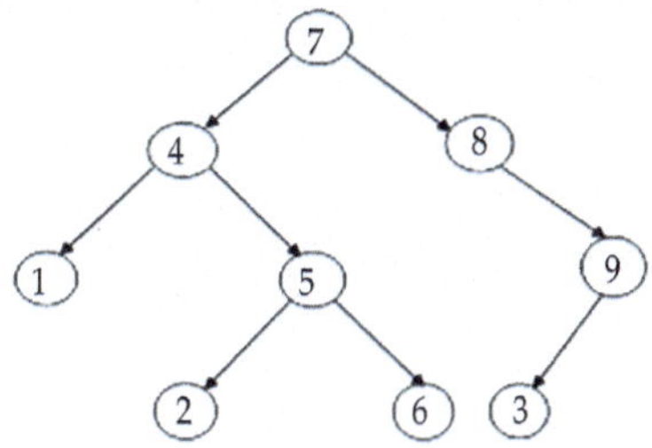

Figure 9.6. Binary tree.

The similar way on the top of the tree is the root which consists of individual elements called the nodes. The nodes which evolve from this root are called the children and every child node in the tree has only one parent.

The root is an exception, which has no parent. The number of children that a node can accommodate depends on the type of the tree. In this section the type of tree that will be under focus will be the binary tree which is a fairly uncomplicated yet pretty powerful.

The reason that it is undemanding and simple can be attributed to the fact that it has a branching factor of only two. That is to say, any parent node can give birth to only two child nodes. A binary tree is a hierarchical representation of nodes with each node giving rise to two nodes. The different levels of hierarchy in the trees can be termed as the siblings, descendants, and ancestors. The siblings of a node are the other nodes of the parent whereas the descendants are the rest of the nodes that follow a particular node. The ancestors of a node are all the nodes that fall in between the path of the root and the node.

Every node in a binary tree can be subdivided into four parts:

- The info;
- Left pointer;
- Right pointer;
- Info Left Right.

The info area as you are aware contains information about the value to be stored in the node and the left pointer points to the left child node and the right pointer points to the right child node. If a node is devoid of children then a null is present in the left and right pointers.

Thus, a binary tree can be represented as follows: Root Null Null Null Null Null Null Null Different traversal methods Traversing as you know, means searching through the list, visiting individual nodes in the process.

In comparison with a few of the linked data structures the method of traversing the nodes of a binary tree may not be instantly apparent. There are four different methods by which traversing a binary tree can be accomplished. - Preorder traversal - In order traversal Element to be inserted.

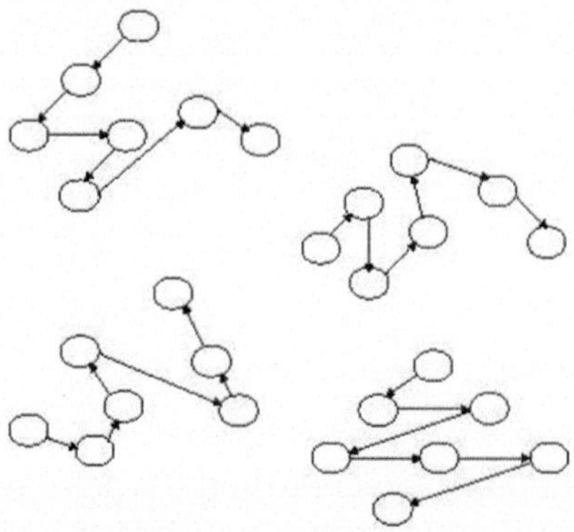

9.8.1. Preorder

The traversal of a binary tree starts with visiting the root node and then traversing the left subtree of its root node in preorder followed by the right subtree in preorder. The preorder traversal is a depth first exploration. Inorder In this type of traversal the left subtree of the root node is traversed in inorder then visit the root node and traverse the right subtree Postorder For traversing a binary tree in post order method the left subhtree of the root node is traversed followed by the right subtree of the root node.

9.8.2. Level-Order

In the level-order the nodes are visited hierarchical level wise from left to right. That is, first the root node is visited. Then both the child nodes of the root are visited starting from the left node following up to the right node and then the child nodes of the left child are visited.

Thus diagrammatically all the four nodes can be represented as follows:

19 78 52 10 14 4 8 19 4 78 8 52 10 14 19 52 79 10 4 14 8 19 78 52 10 14 8 4

9.9. SORTING TECHNIQUES-I

Just imagine trying to trace out a word from a dictionary which is not arranged in an alphabetical fashion. Impossible. Try tracing out a book in a library where the books are not indexed. Nerve wracking. These are just a few examples where things have to be sorted for saving a lot of time and energy.

In fact, for a person's life to run smoothly his daily activities c.) Post Order d.) Level a.) Preorder b.) In Order

9.9.1. Order

All through this session you have been mastering the tricks of inserting and deleting elements in various types of data structures. Newer methods were applied and various practices were examined. In all this frenzied rush of piling long lists of numbers the sorting of numbers was ignored. Only when the elements are sorted and arranged can they be presented.

You will now deal with the various methods of sorting the arranged elements. You will be surprised to find that 'C' supports so many methods and it can execute them eloquently and effectively. The sorting method that will be dealt with in this session give a representative sample of the most popular techniques used.

Sorting methods taken up here, vary in their degree of intensity. Where a couple of methods are trivial on the other hand complex yet efficient sorting techniques have also gained entry into the session. Before getting acquainted with the various sorting operations, let us be clear what sorting exactly is. Sorting is a process of arranging the records of a table or the elements of a list in some sequential order according to a particular criterion.

The various types of sorting technique that you will undertake here are:

- Selection sort;
- Bubble sort;
- Merge sort;
- Heap sort;
- Quick sort;
- Radix sort.

9.9.2. Selection Sort

The selection sort can be termed easily as the most undemanding method of those mentioned above where elements are arranged in an ascending order. Consider a set of elements that have to be sorted.

41, 22, 73, 10, 64, 57, 93, 35, 98, 86

When these elements are arranged in a list they will bear the following positions:

1 2 3 4 5 6 7 8 9 10 42 22 73 10 64 57 93 35 98 86

When a selection sort process starts, the smallest element is selected and it is compared with the element in the first position.

If the smallest element is less than the other one the elements are swapped. In the above example the smallest element in the list is 10. This element is compared with the element in the first position which is 41 and since the smallest number is less than 41 their positions are swapped. As a next step, the second smallest number is compared with the element in the second position and they are swapped.

Then the third smallest is compared with the element in third position and so on until all the elements are arranged in an ascending order. have to be sorted according to priorities. The BELL laboratories had incorporated this human technology into C. when you have scores and scores of numbers to tackle it would definitely be comfortable and time effective if the numbers are sorted in a particular order to ensure efficiency of results.

In this session, C offers a wide range of options for you to choose from so that the most convenient method may be applied to sort a given set of elements. The techniques listed below vary in their degree of intensity but all of them are extremely effective in their own right (Figure 9.7).

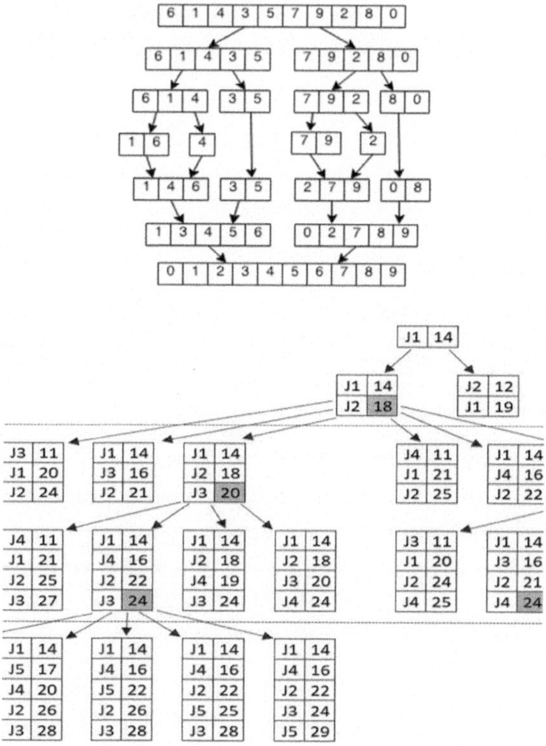

Figure 9.7. Sorting techniques.

When a selection sort process starts, the smallest element is selected and it is compared with the element in the first position. If the smallest element is less than the other one the elements are swapped. In the above example the smallest element in the list is 10. This element is compared with the element in the first position which is 41 and since the smallest number is less than 41 their positions are swapped.

As a next step, the second smallest number is compared with the element in the second position and they are swapped. Then the third smallest is compared with the element in third position and so on until all the elements are arranged in an ascending order. Merge sorting The earlier two methods of sorting were relatively simple.

There was no dichotomy of the list or any such complication. This method is recursive and fairly simple to comprehend. It involves the performing of a merge sort on two different ordered lists. Both the lists are merged to form a new ordered list.

For a merge sort to be conducted successfully apart from two ordered lists a third list is also required whose size is equal to the sum of the two lists.

For example if a list x has 3 elements and another list y has 2 then the third empty list should have a size of 5 so that it can accommodate all the elements of both the lists.

Consider 2 lists x and y with elements 1 2 3 X 20 50 100 1 2 Y 5 45 Z 1 2 3 4 5

Now the merge sort is performed in such a way that in the first comparison the elements in the 1st position of both the lists are compared and the smaller element is assigned the first position in the list z.

Hence in the above lists 5 and 20 compared and 5 is entered in the first position of z. 1 2 3 4 5 Z 5. Here i and j are two pointers. Now since the element in y has been removed the pointer j is incremented and it points to the 2nd position. Now y2 is compared with x1 and the smaller value assigned to z. In this case 20 will occupy the 2nd position in z and the i pointer is incremented.

The comparisons are done in such a fashion and the elements in both the list x and y are empty and a sorted list is available in z. Thus, after merge sort the list z can be represented as follows:

1 2 3 4 5 5 20 45 50 100

9.10. SORTING TECHNIQUES-II

The above discussed sorting methods may have been elementary to you but don't pass your verdict too soon, because the bad boys are yet to invade.

In second saga of the sorting techniques, methods which are a bit complex but highly effective are taken up and split according to their priority modules. Heap sort Heap sort is just another dull boring sort method you may think but this is one those of those offbeat ones.

Say you have a situation where only the smallest and the largest element of the list has to be found out.

There are two approaches: first, sort the full list, then show the smallest and biggest element.

Use heap sort and directly find the least and largest element.

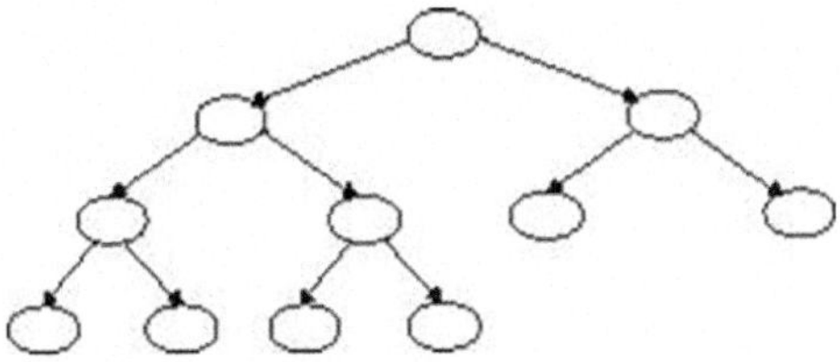

Obviously the latter option is advisable because if you have a large list and you use the former method you will end up forfeiting a lot of time and resources. A heap is a tree most often referred as a binary tree. The difference between the heap and any other tree in a heap every child node has a value which is less than its parent value. Thus, the root node is the node with the largest value.

The above approach is called top-heavy where although the nodes along every branch has a particular order the nodes at a level are not necessarily ordered. If the above approach is not particularly appealing then the heaps offer another method called bottom-heavy in which the root node is the smallest in the list and the parent node is essentially less than the child nodes. As the nodes are added they grow from left to right.

The most approved method is to store nodes successively in an array in the pattern one would encounter them in a level traversal. Consider a zero-indexed array, that is the parent of each node at a position I in the array is located at position(I-1)/2. The left and right children of a node are situated at the positions 2I+1 and 2I+2. Using this kind of arrangement it is easy to locate a heap's last node because the right most node at the deepest level is the last node.

24 21 19 11 10 18 16 17 8 6 14 0 1 2 3 4 5 6 7 8 9 1 0 24 19 8 6 14 11 9 18 16 21

Quick sort – the quick sort mechanism can also be termed as partition exchange sort.

The main reason behind giving it the name partition exchange sort lies in the very essence that this program is based on placing a specific element at the right position in each partition. The flow of the process begins by taking a pivot element.

A pivot element is always the first element of the list. Now, the pivot element must be placed at one of the positions in the list in such a manner that all the elements towards the left of pivot element are less than it and all the elements towards the right are greater than it.

For example in the given set of numbers:

30, 12, 16, 11, 24, 35, 56, 51, 45 35 is the pivot element which is placed as per the mentioned example. This way, the whole list is partitioned into two sub-lists, one which is less than or equal to pivot element and the other, which is greater than or equal to the pivot element.

Now each partition will have its own pivot element which will be assigned to the first element in the partition. The partitions are further divided into sub-partitions to have their own pivot elements, until each partition has either one element or null towards left or right.

Once all the portions have been successfully sorted, all the portions are united to form a sorted list. Let us consider the given list of numbers which have to be sorted using the quick sort method. 35,56,51,45,30,12,16,11,24. Now, the first element 35 is designated the pivot element. 35 is compared with the remaining list towards the right until it reaches the first element less than itself (in this case 30).

Now let us assign this position a variable x. Theelement at position x is 30 and it takes the position of the pivot element. All the elements from the pivot element till the element at position (x-1) are moved up the order such that the vacant space at position x is filled.

Hence, you obtain the list as follows:

30,35,56,51,45,12,16,11,24

The same process continues until all the elements toward right of the pivot element are greater than itself.

- **Step 1:** 30, 12, 35, 56, 51, 45, 16, 11, 24.
- **Step 2:** 30, 12, 16, 35, 56, 51, 45, 11, 24.
- **Step 3:** 30, 12, 16, 11, 35, 56, 51, 45, 24.
- **Step 4:** 30, 12, 16, 11, 24, 35, 56, 51, 45.

Therefore you have obtained the list that was given to you as an example in the beginning of the topic, now all the elements towards left are identified as one portion having 30 as their new pivot element. And all the elements towards right are identified to be next portion having 56 as their new pivot element.

{30, 12, 16, 11, 24} 35 {56, 51, 45}

Now each partition is independently sorted as follows.

- **Step 1:** {12, 30, 16, 11, 24} 35 {56, 51, 45}

- **Step 2:** {12, 16, 30, 11, 24} 35 {51, 56, 45}
- **Step 3:** {12, 16, 11, 30, 24} 35 {51, 45, 56}
- **Step 4:** {12, 16, 11, 24, 30} 35 {51, 45, 56}

Therefore the new list with partition is obtained as follows.

- **Step 1:** {[12, 16, 11, 24] 30} 35 {[51, 45] 56}
- **Step 2:** {[11, 12, 16, 24] 30} 35 {[45, 51] 56}

Hence you obtain a list:

11, 12, 16, 24, 30, 35, 45, 51, 56.

9.10.1. Radix Sort

The radix sort can be declared as the most efficient sorting methods available. It is generally applicable for 2 digit numbers but the concept holds good even for 3 digit numbers though the examples dealt with here are only using two digit numbers.

This version of the sorting technique is pretty simple and involves in dividing every element into two parts. The right digit or the digit in the tens place is called most significant digit (MSD) and digit in the units place is called least significant digit (LSD). Example: in the number 40 the LSD and the MSD are demarcated as follows:

MSD: 4 LSD: 0

The whole sorting process is carried out on the basis of sorting the LSD and MSD. The whole radix sort process is two step procedure where the sorting in the first step is based on lsd and sorting in second is based on msd.

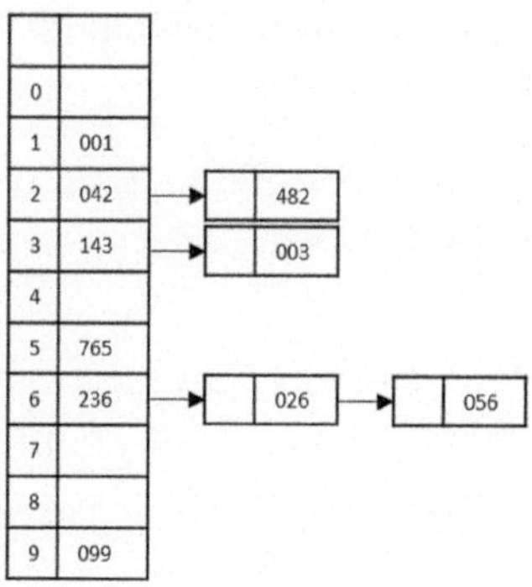

Consider the list of elements:

40, 45, 61, 72, 67, 89, 98, 50, 57

To sort the element the radix sort involves a group of pockets which are numbered from 0 to 9.

These pockets can accept numbers whose lsd is equal to the respective pocket numbers.

For example 0th pocket can accommodate only elements that end with 0. Similarly, pocket no 5 accommodates elements whose lsd is 5 and each pocket can accommodate only one element per pass Step I In the first step the list is traversed and elements are placed in the pockets based on their lsd.

Once an element is placed in its respective pocket of another element with the same lsd is encountered it is ignored until the rest of the list is scanned. This scanning through a list once is called a pass.

For example in the above list you have two elements 40 and 50 having lsd as 0. In the first pass only 40 is placed in the 0th pocket since it is encountered first. The 50 is placed in the 0th pocket in the second pass.

Hence after the completion of the first step the elements can be represented as follows: P

0 40 50 1 61 2 72 3 4 5 45 6 7 67 57 8 9

Now based on the arrangement a new list is prepared as follows:

40, 50, 61, 72, 45, 67, 57

You will notice that while a list is prepared the element in the 2nd pass slides beside the element in the 1st pass.

This list of elements is now used as fuel for the second step.

Step II is similar to Step I with a variation that these elements are entered into their respective pockets based on the msd. 0 1 2 3 4 40 45 5 50 57 6 61 67 7 72 8 9. Hence the new ordered list can be represented as follows:

40, 45, 50, 57, 61, 67, 72.

After having dealt with the various sorting techniques it is difficult to judge which technique is the most superior one. Though some are easy to use it may not really be effective.

Certain properties of a given key set play an important role in the determination of which sorting technique should be used. The properties are the number, size, distribution, and order of keys. Often decide which method will be apt in a situation.

9.11. SEARCHING TECHNIQUES

The techniques used by you till now were helpful in arranging elements in different ways and means. Now that the list is sorted and arranged it is retrieval time. The searching techniques that you will now experience allows you to dig out an element of your choice from the list. The element of your choice is compared with the elements of the list and if a perfect match is found then the element is retrieved and a message is displayed.

The searching process can be done in different ways but the most popular will be taken up and dissected. C allows two major and uncomplicated means of searching elements.

1. **Linear Search Method:** The linear method is a fairly straightforward method of retrieving elements. This is often considered the simplest technique for searching an unordered list of elements.

   In the following version the list is scanned element by element for the element to be retrieved. When an appropriate match is found a message is displayed.

2. **Binary Search Method:** This is another relatively simple method of accessing a list of elements. An important point to be kept in mind that the binary search is possible only if the list of elements is ordered and in an ascending manner. This can be achieved by applying any of the sorting technique available in the early part of the session.

Once the list is aligned the binary search operation can proceed. this method the list is assigned a lower bound and an upper bound to the 1st and the last element. After this is done the midpoint of the list is found by finding the average of the lb and the ub. For example, if the list contains 7 elements then the midpoint will be 4 Midpoint=lb+ub/2. Consider the list of elements below and say the element to be retrieved is 91. 40, 55, 61, 71, 81, 91, 100. Once the midpoint is found the element to be searched is compared with the element present in the position of the midpoint.

In this case the element present at the midpoint is 71. The element 71 is compared with the sought after element which is 91 but since the elements differ in configuration the element is checked if it is greater than or less than the midpoint.

If the element is less than the midpoint the rest of the searching takes place with the elements on the left side of the midpoint since all those elements are less than the midpoint. If the number is larger than the midpoint then the comparison takes place with the elements on the right of the midpoint.

In your case since the element is larger than the midpoint the latter situation will be of concern. After it is decided that the element is larger the element after the midpoint is assigned the position of the lower bound but the upper bound remains the same. In the contrasting case if the element is less than the element before the mid is made as the upper bound, but that is not the case here.

Now that you have a new lower bound in the above case the midpoint of the new lb and the ub are found out. Thus, in this case it would be 6 (5+7/2). The new midpoint is now compared with the element to be searched. Since a perfect match is found a message is displayed that the search is complete and the desired element is found.

If still a match is not found the above method is continued until a bulls eye is hit.

9.11.1. Practical Approaches

- **Practical 1:** Installation C IDE, Basic Structure of C program. Format Specifiers, Escape Character. Run time input/output Programs.
- **Solution:**

Installing a C IDE:

There are several Integrated Development Environments (IDEs) available for C programming. One popular option is Code::Blocks. Here's how you can install Code::Blocks on a Windows system:

1. **Download Code::Blocks:**

- Visit the official Code::Blocks website: http://www.codeblocks.org/
- Go to the "Downloads" section.
- Download the appropriate version for your operating system (Windows, Linux, etc.).

2. **Install Code::Blocks:**

- Run the installer you downloaded.
- Follow the on-screen instructions to complete the installation.

3. **Open Code::Blocks:**

- Once installed, open Code::Blocks.

9.11.2. Basic Structure of a C Program

```
// Preprocessor Directives
#include <stdio.h> // Include necessary libraries
// Main Function
int main()
{
// Declarations (Variable and Function Declarations)
// Statements (Executable code)
return 0; // Return statement (Exit status)
}
```

- **Preprocessor Directives:** These lines begin with # and are used to include libraries and perform other pre-processing tasks.
- **main():** This is the main function where program execution begins.
- **Declarations:** This is where you declare variables and functions that will be used in your program.
- **Statements:** These are the executable statements that perform the actual work of your program.
- **return 0;:** This line is used to exit the program with a status code of 0, indicating successful execution.

9.11.3. Format Specifiers

Format specifiers are used in C to specify the data type of the variables you want to print or read using functions like printf and scanf. Common format specifiers include:

- %d: Integer
- %f: Float or double
- %c: Character
- %s: String

9.11.4. Escape Characters

Escape characters are used to represent special characters within strings or characters. Some common escape characters include:

- "\": Double quote
- '\': Single quote
- \\: Backslash
- \n: Newline
- \t: Tab

9.11.5. Runtime Input/Output Programs

```
#include <stdio.h>
int main()
{
int age;
char name[50];
printf("Enter your name: ");
scanf("%s", name); // Read a string (no spaces)
printf("Enter your age: ");
scanf("%d", &age); // Read an integer
printf("Hello, %s! You are %d years old.\n", name, age);
return 0;
}
```

- **Practical 2:** A basic example of a C program that prints "Hello, World!" to the console.
- **Solution:**

```
#include <stdio.h>
int main()
{
printf("Hello, World!\n");
return 0;
}
```

Let me break down the key components of this program:

- #include <stdio.h>: This line includes the standard input/output library, which provides functions like printf for printing to the console.
- int main(): This is the starting point of the program. Every C program must have a main function, and execution begins here. int is the return type, which indicates that the main function will return an integer value when it completes.
- {}: These curly braces enclose the body of the main function, where the program's statements are placed.
- printf("Hello, World!\n");: This line uses the printf function to print the text "Hello, World!" to the console. \n represents a newline character, which moves the cursor to the next line.
- return 0;: This line returns an integer value of 0 to indicate that the program has executed without any errors. In C, a return value of 0 conventionally signifies success.

To compile and run this program, you'll need a C compiler installed on your system, such as GCC. Save the code to a file with a.c extension (e.g., hello.c), and then use the following commands to compile and run it:

- **Output:**

```
gcc hello.c-o hello # Compile the program
./hello # Run the compiled program
```

- **Practical 3:** Write a c program to calculate Area of Rectangle, Perimeter of a Rectangle and Diagonal of a Rectangle.
- **Solution:**

```
#include <stdio.h>
#include <math.h>
int main()
{
double length, width, area, perimeter, diagonal;
// Input the length and width of the rectangle
printf("Enter the length of the rectangle: ");
scanf("%lf", &length);
printf("Enter the width of the rectangle: ");
scanf("%lf", &width);
```

```
// Calculate the area, perimeter, and diagonal
area = length * width;
perimeter = 2 * (length + width);
diagonal = sqrt(length * length + width * width);
// Display the results
printf("Area of the rectangle: %.2lf\n", area);
printf("Perimeter of the rectangle: %.2lf\n", perimeter);
printf("Diagonal of the rectangle: %.2lf\n", diagonal);
return 0;
}
```

- **Practical 4:** Write a c program to calculate Area of square, Perimeter of a square and Diagonal of a square.
- **Solution:**

```
#include <stdio.h>
#include <math.h>
int main()
{
double side, area, perimeter, diagonal;
// Input the side length of the square
printf("Enter the side length of the square: ");
scanf("%lf", &side);
// Calculate the area, perimeter, and diagonal
area = side * side;
perimeter = 4 * side;
diagonal = side * sqrt(2);
// Display the results
printf("Area of the square: %.2lf\n", area);
printf("Perimeter of the square: %.2lf\n", perimeter);
printf("Diagonal of the square: %.2lf\n", diagonal);
return 0;
}
```

- **Practical 5:** Write a c program to calculate total area of Cylinder and volume of a cylinder.

- **Solution:**

```
#include <stdio.h>
#include <math.h>
int main()
{
double radius, height;
double pi = 3.14159265359; // Approximate value of Pi
// Input the radius and height of the cylinder
printf("Enter the radius of the cylinder: ");
scanf("%lf", &radius);
printf("Enter the height of the cylinder: ");
scanf("%lf", &height);
// Calculate the total surface area of the cylinder
double surface_area = 2 * pi * radius * (radius + height);
// Calculate the volume of the cylinder
double volume = pi * pow(radius, 2) * height;
// Display the results
printf("Total surface area of the cylinder: %.2lf square units\n", surface_
area);
printf("Volume of the cylinder: %.2lf cubic units\n", volume);
return 0;
}
```

- **Practical 6:** The total distance traveled by vehicle in t seconds is given by distance s = ut+1/2at? where 'u' and 'a' are the initial velocity (m/sec.) and acceleration(m/sec?). Write a C program to find the distance traveled at regular intervals of time given the values of 'u' and 'a' The program should provide the flexibility to the user to select his own time intervals and repeat the calculations for different values of 'u' and 'a.'

```
#include <stdio.h>
int main()
{
```

```
double u, a, t, distance;
int num_intervals;
printf("Enter initial velocity (u) in m/sec: ");
scanf("%lf", &u);
printf("Enter acceleration (a) in m/sec^2: ");
scanf("%lf", &a);
printf("Enter the number of time intervals: ");
scanf("%d", &num_intervals);
for (int i = 1; i <= num_intervals; i++)
{
printf("Enter time interval %d in seconds: ", i);
scanf("%lf", &t);
distance = u * t + 0.5 * a * t * t;
printf("Distance traveled at time %.2lf seconds: %.2lf meters\n", t, distance);
}
return 0;
}
```

- **Practical 7:** Write a C program, which takes two integer operands and one operator from the user, performs the operation and then prints the result. (Consider the operators +,-,",/,% and use Switch Statement)
- **Solution:**

```
#include <stdio.h>
int main()
{
int operand1, operand2;
char operator;
printf("Enter two integer operands: ");
scanf("%d %d", &operand1, &operand2);
printf("Enter an operator (+, –, *, /, %%): ");
scanf(" %c", &operator); // Notice the space before %c to consume any
```

leading whitespace.

switch (operator)

{

case ‘+’:

printf(“Result: %d + %d = %d\n”, operand1, operand2, operand1 + operand2);

break;

case ‘-’:

printf(“Result: %d – %d = %d\n”, operand1, operand2, operand1 – operand2);

break;

case ‘*’:

printf(“Result: %d * %d = %d\n”, operand1, operand2, operand1 * operand2);

break;

case ‘/’:

if (operand2 != 0)

{

printf(“Result: %d / %d = %.2lf\n”, operand1, operand2, (double) operand1 / operand2);

}

else

{

printf(“Error: Division by zero is not allowed.\n”);

}

break;

case ‘%’:

if (operand2 != 0)

{

printf(“Result: %d %% %d = %d\n”, operand1, operand2, operand1 % operand2);

}

```
else
{
printf("Error: Modulo by zero is not allowed.\n");
}
break;
default:
printf("Error: Invalid operator entered.\n");
}
return 0;
}
```

- **Practical 8:** Write a C program to find the sum of individual digits of a positive integer.
- **Solution:**

```
#include <stdio.h>
int main()
{
int num, sum = 0, digit;
// Input a positive integer
printf("Enter a positive integer: ");
scanf("%d", &num);
// Check if the input is a positive integer
if (num < 0)
{
printf("Please enter a positive integer.\n");
return 1; // Exit with an error code
}
// Calculate the sum of individual digits
while (num > 0)
{
digit = num % 10; // Get the last digit
sum += digit; // Add the digit to the sum
num /= 10; // Remove the last digit
```

```
}
// Display the sum of digits
printf("The sum of individual digits is: %d\n", sum);
return 0; // Exit successfully
}
```

- **Practical 9:** A Fibonacci sequence is defined as follows: the first and second terms in the sequences are 0 and 1. Subsequent terms are found by adding the preceding two terms in the sequence. Write a C program to generate the first n terms of the sequence.
- **Solution:**

```
#include <stdio.h>
int main()
{
int n, first = 0, second = 1, next, i;
// Input the number of terms to generate
printf("Enter the number of terms: ");
scanf("%d", &n);
// Check if n is valid
if (n <= 0)
{
printf("Please enter a positive integer for the number of terms.\n");
return 1; // Exit with an error code
}
// Print the first two terms (0 and 1) manually
printf("Fibonacci Series: %d, %d", first, second);
// Generate and print the rest of the terms
for (i = 2; i < n; i++)
{
next = first + second;
printf(", %d", next);
first = second;
second = next;
```

```
}
printf("\n");
return 0; // Exit successfully
}
```

- **Practical 10:** Write a C program to generate all the prime numbers between 1 and n, where n is a value supplied by the user.
- **Solution:**

```
#include <stdio.h>
int is_prime(int num)
{
if (num <= 1)
{
return 0; // 0 and 1 are not prime numbers
}
for (int i = 2; i * i <= num; i++)
{
if (num % i == 0)
{
return 0; // It's divisible by a number other than 1 and itself
}
}
return 1; // It's a prime number
}
int main()
{
int n;
// Input the value of n
printf("Enter a positive integer n: ");
scanf("%d", &n);
// Check if n is valid
if (n <= 1)
{
```

```
printf("Please enter a positive integer greater than 1.\n");
return 1; // Exit with an error code
}
printf("Prime numbers between 1 and %d are:\n", n);
// Generate and print prime numbers between 1 and n
for (int i = 2; i <= n; i++)
{
if (is_prime(i))
{
printf("%d ", i);
}
}
printf("\n");
return 0; // Exit successfully
}
```

- **Practical 11:** Write a C program to calculate the following Sum: Sum=1-x^2/2! +x^4/4!-x^6/6!+x^8/8!-x^10/10!.
- **Solution:**

```
#include <stdio.h>
#include <math.h>
int main()
{
double x;
int n;
double sum = 1.0;
// Input the value of x and the number of terms (n)
printf("Enter the value of x: ");
scanf("%lf", &x);
printf("Enter the number of terms (n): ");
scanf("%d", &n);
// Calculate and print the sum
for (int i = 1; i <= n; i++)
```

```
{
double term = pow(-1, i) * pow(x, 2 * i) / (2 * i);
sum += term;
}
printf("The sum is: %lf\n", sum);
return 0; // Exit successfully
}
```

- **Practical 12:** Write a C program to find the roots of a quadratic equation.
- **Solution:**

```
#include <stdio.h>
#include <math.h>
int main()
{
double a, b, c;
double discriminant, root1, root2;
// Input coefficients a, b, and c
printf("Enter coefficient a: ");
scanf("%lf", &a);
printf("Enter coefficient b: ");
scanf("%lf", &b);
printf("Enter coefficient c: ");
scanf("%lf", &c);
// Calculate the discriminant
discriminant = b * b – 4 * a * c;
// Check the value of the discriminant
if (discriminant > 0)
{
// Two real and distinct roots
root1 = (-b + sqrt(discriminant)) / (2 * a);
root2 = (–b – sqrt(discriminant)) / (2 * a);
printf("Root 1 = %.2lf and Root 2 = %.2lf\n", root1, root2);
```

```
}
else if (discriminant == 0)
{
// One real root (repeated)
root1 = –b / (2 * a);
printf("Root 1 = Root 2 = %.2lf\n", root1);
}
else
{
// Complex roots
double realPart = –b / (2 * a);
double imaginaryPart = sqrt(-discriminant) / (2 * a);
printf("Root 1 = %.2lf + %.2lfi and Root 2 = %.2lf – %.2lfi\n", realPart,
imaginaryPart, realPart, imaginaryPart);
}
return 0; // Exit successfully
}
```

- **Practical 13:** To find the factorial of a given integer.
- **Solution:**

```
#include <stdio.h>
int main()
{
int n;
unsigned long long factorial = 1;
// Input the integer for which you want to find the factorial
printf("Enter a non-negative integer: ");
scanf("%d", &n);
// Check if n is negative
if (n < 0)
{
printf("Factorial is not defined for negative integers.\n");
return 1; // Exit with an error code
```

```
}
// Calculate the factorial
for (int i = 1; i <= n; i++)
{
factorial *= i;
}
// Print the factorial
printf("%d! = %llu\n", n, factorial);
return 0; // Exit successfully
}
```

- **Practical 14:** To find the GCD (greatest common divisor) of two given integers.
- **Solution:**

```
#include <stdio.h>
// Function to calculate the GCD using the Euclidean algorithm
int gcd(int a, int b)
{
if (b == 0)
{
return a;
}
return gcd(b, a % b);
}
int main()
{
int num1, num2;
// Input the two integers
printf("Enter the first integer: ");
scanf("%d", &num1);
printf("Enter the second integer: ");
scanf("%d", &num2);
// Calculate and print the GCD
```

```
int result = gcd(num1, num2);
printf("The GCD of %d and %d is: %d\n", num1, num2, result);
return 0; // Exit successfully
}
```

- **Practical 15:** Write a C program to find the largest integer in a list of integers.
- **Solution:**

```
#include <stdio.h>
int main()
{
int n; // Number of integers in the list
printf("Enter the number of integers: ");
scanf("%d", &n);
if (n <= 0)
{
printf("Invalid input. Please enter a positive number.\n");
return 1; // Exit with an error code
}
int largest; // Variable to store the largest integer
int current; // Variable to store the current integer
// Prompt the user to enter the first integer
printf("Enter integer 1: ");
scanf("%d", &largest);
for (int i = 2; i <= n; i++)
{
// Prompt the user to enter the next integer
printf("Enter integer %d: ", i);
scanf("%d", &current);
// Check if the current integer is larger than the largest
if (current > largest)
{
largest = current; // Update the largest integer
```

```
}
}
// Print the largest integer
printf("The largest integer is: %d\n", largest);
return 0; // Exit successfully
}
```

- **Practical 16:** Write a C program that uses functions to perform the following:
  1. Addition of two matrices;
  2. Multiplication of two matrices.
- **Solution:**

```
#include <stdio.h>
#define MAX_ROWS 10
#define MAX_COLS 10
void inputMatrix(int matrix[MAX_ROWS][MAX_COLS], int rows, int cols)
{
printf("Enter matrix elements row by row:\n");
for (int i = 0; i < rows; i++)
{
for (int j = 0; j < cols; j++)
{
printf("Enter element at row %d, column %d: ", i + 1, j + 1);
scanf("%d", &matrix[i][j]);
}
}
}
void printMatrix(int matrix[MAX_ROWS][MAX_COLS], int rows, int cols)
{
printf("Matrix:\n");
for (int i = 0; i < rows; i++)
```

```
{
for (int j = 0; j < cols; j++)
{
printf("%d\t", matrix[i][j]);
}
printf("\n");
}
}
void addMatrices(int A[MAX_ROWS][MAX_COLS], int B[MAX_ROWS][MAX_COLS], int C[MAX_ROWS][MAX_COLS], int rows, int cols)
{
for (int i = 0; i < rows; i++)
{
for (int j = 0; j < cols; j++)
{
C[i][j] = A[i][j] + B[i][j];
}
}
}
void multiplyMatrices(int A[MAX_ROWS][MAX_COLS], int B[MAX_ROWS][MAX_COLS], int C[MAX_ROWS][MAX_COLS], int rows1, int cols1, int cols2)
{
for (int i = 0; i < rows1; i++)
{
for (int j = 0; j < cols2; j++)
{
C[i][j] = 0;
for (int k = 0; k < cols1; k++)
{
C[i][j] += A[i][k] * B[k][j];
```

```
}
}
}
}
int main()
{
int rows1, cols1, rows2, cols2;
printf("Enter the number of rows and columns for matrix A: ");
scanf("%d %d", &rows1, &cols1);
printf("Enter the number of rows and columns for matrix B: ");
scanf("%d %d", &rows2, &cols2);
if (rows1 != rows2 || cols1 != cols2)
{
printf("Matrix addition and multiplication are not possible. The matrices
must have the same dimensions.\n");
return 1;
}
int matrixA[MAX_ROWS][MAX_COLS];
int matrixB[MAX_ROWS][MAX_COLS];
int resultMatrix[MAX_ROWS][MAX_COLS];
printf("Matrix A:\n");
inputMatrix(matrixA, rows1, cols1);
printf("Matrix B:\n");
inputMatrix(matrixB, rows2, cols2);
// Perform matrix addition
addMatrices(matrixA, matrixB, resultMatrix, rows1, cols1);
printf("Matrix Addition Result:\n");
printMatrix(resultMatrix, rows1, cols1);
// Perform matrix multiplication
if (cols1 != rows2)
{
```

```
printf("Matrix multiplication is not possible. The number of columns in matrix A must be equal to the number of rows in matrix B.\n");
return 1;
}
multiplyMatrices(matrixA, matrixB, resultMatrix, rows1, cols1, cols2);
printf("Matrix Multiplication Result:\n");
printMatrix(resultMatrix, rows1, cols2);
return 0;
}
```

- **Practical 17:** Write a C program that uses functions to perform the following operation;

1. To insert a sub-string into a given main string from a given position.
2. To delete n Characters from a given position in a given string,

- **Solution:**

```
#include <stdio.h>
#include <string.h>
void insertSubstring(char *mainStr, char *subStr, int position)
{
int mainLen = strlen(mainStr);
int subLen = strlen(subStr);
if (position < 0 || position > mainLen)
{
printf("Invalid position for insertion\n");
return;
}
memmove(mainStr + position + subLen, mainStr + position, mainLen – position + 1);
strncpy(mainStr + position, subStr, subLen);
}
void deleteCharacters(char *str, int position, int n)
{
```

```
int strLen = strlen(str);
if (position < 0 || position >= strLen || n < 0)
{
printf("Invalid position or number of characters to delete\n");
return;
}
memmove(str + position, str + position + n, strLen – position – n + 1);
}
int main()
{
char mainStr[100];
char subStr[50];
int position, n;
printf("Enter a main string: ");
scanf("%s", mainStr);
printf("Enter a substring to insert: ");
scanf("%s", subStr);
printf("Enter the position to insert the substring: ");
scanf("%d", &position);
insertSubstring(mainStr, subStr, position);
printf("Result after insertion: %s\n", mainStr);
printf("Enter the position to start deletion: ");
scanf("%d", &position);
printf("Enter the number of characters to delete: ");
scanf("%d", &n);
deleteCharacters(mainStr, position, n);
printf("Result after deletion: %s\n", mainStr);
return 0;
}
```

- **Practical 18:** Write a C program to determine if the given string is a palindrome or not.
- **Solution:**

```
#include <stdio.h>
#include <stdbool.h>
#include <string.h>
bool isPalindrome(char *str)
{
int len = strlen(str);
int i, j;
for (i = 0, j = len – 1; i < j; i++, j--)
{
if (str[i] != str[j])
{
return false;
}
}
return true;
}
int main()
{
char str[100];
printf("Enter a string: ");
scanf("%s", str);
if (isPalindrome(str))
{
printf("%s is a palindrome.\n", str);
}
else
{
printf("%s is not a palindrome.\n", str);
}
return 0;
}
```

- **Practical 19:** Write a C program that displays the position or index in the string S where the string T begins, or –1 if S doesn't contain T.
- **Solution:**

```
#include <stdio.h>
#include <string.h>
int findSubstringIndex(const char *S, const char *T)
{
int sLen = strlen(S);
int tLen = strlen(T);
for (int i = 0; i <= sLen – tLen; i++)
{
int j;
for (j = 0; j < tLen; j++)
{
if (S[i + j] != T[j])
{
break;
}
}
if (j == tLen)
{
return i; // Found the substring
}
}
return –1; // Substring not found
}
int main()
{
const char *S = "Hello, World!";
const char *T = "World";
int index = findSubstringIndex(S, T);
```

```
if (index ! = –1)
{
printf("Substring found at index %d\n", index);
}
else
{
printf("Substring not found\n");
}
return 0;
}
```

- **Practical 20:** Write a C program to count the lines, words, and characters in a given text.
- **Solution:**

```
#include <stdio.h>
#include <stdbool.h>
// Function to count lines, words, and characters
void countLinesWordsChars(const char *text, int *lines, int *words, int
*characters)
{
*lines = 0;
*words = 0;
*characters = 0;
bool inWord = false; // Flag to track if we are inside a word
for (int i = 0; text[i] != '\0'; i++)
{
(*characters)++; // Increment character count
// Check for newline character to count lines
if (text[i] == '\n')
{
(*lines)++;
}
// Check for whitespace or newline to detect words
```

```
if (text[i] == ' ' || text[i] == '\t' || text[i] == '\n')
{
inWord = false;
}
else if (!inWord)
{
(*words)++;
inWord = true;
}
}
// If the last character is not a newline, increment the line count
if (text[*characters – 1] != '\n')
{
(*lines)++;
}
}
int main()
{
const char *text = "This is a sample text.\nIt has multiple lines and words.";
int lines, words, characters;
countLinesWordsChars(text, &lines, &words, &characters);
printf("Lines: %d\n", lines);
printf("Words: %d\n", words);
printf("Characters: %d\n", characters);
return 0;
}
```

- **Practical 21:** Write a C program to generate Pascal's triangle.
- **Solution:**

```
#include <stdio.h>
// Function to calculate the factorial of a number
unsigned long long factorial(int n)
```

```
{
if (n <= 1)
{
return 1;
}
else
{
return n * factorial(n – 1);
}
}
// Function to calculate and print Pascal's triangle
void generatePascalsTriangle(int numRows)
{
for (int i = 0; i < numRows; i++)
{
for (int j = 0; j <= (numRows – i – 2); j++)
{
printf(" "); // Print spaces for formatting
}
for (int j = 0; j <= i; j++)
{
// Calculate and print the binomial coefficient
unsigned long long coefficient = factorial(i) / (factorial(j) * factorial(i
–j));
printf("%6llu ", coefficient);
}
printf("\n");
}
}
int main()
{
```

```
int numRows;
printf("Enter the number of rows for Pascal's triangle: ");
scanf("%d", &numRows);
generatePascalsTriangle(numRows);
return 0;
}
```

- **Practical 22:** Write a C program to construct a pyramid of numbers.
- **Solution:**

```
#include <stdio.h>
void printPyramid(int rows)
{
for (int i = 1; i <= rows; i++)
{
// Print leading spaces
for (int j = 1; j <= rows – i; j++)
{
printf(" ");
}
// Print increasing numbers
for (int j = 1; j <= i; j++)
{
printf("%d ", j);
}
// Print decreasing numbers
for (int j = i – 1; j >= 1; j--)
{
printf("%d ", j);
}
// Move to the next line
printf("\n");
}
```

```
}
int main()
{
int rows;
printf("Enter the number of rows for the pyramid: ");
scanf("%d", &rows);
printPyramid(rows);
return 0;
}
```

- **Practical 23:** Write a C program to read in two numbers, x and n, and then compute the sum of this geometric progression: 1+x+x^2+x^3+… x^n.
- **Solution:**

```
#include <stdio.h>
#include <math.h>
int main()
{
double x;
int n;
printf("Enter the value of x: ");
scanf("%lf", &x);
printf("Enter the value of n: ");
scanf("%d", &n);
double sum = 0.0;
for (int i = 0; i <= n; i++)
{
sum += pow(x, i);
}
printf("Sum of the geometric progression: %.2lf\n", sum);
return 0;
}
```

- **Practical 24:** 2's complement of a number is obtained by scanning it from right to left and complementing all the bits after the first appearance of a 1. Thus, 2's complement of 11100 is 00100. Write a C program to find the 2's complement of a binary number.

- **Solution:**

```
#include <stdio.h>
#include <string.h>
// Function to reverse a binary string
void reverseBinaryString(char *binary)
{
int len = strlen(binary);
for (int i = 0; i < len / 2; i++)
{
char temp = binary[i];
binary[i] = binary[len – i – 1];
binary[len – i – 1] = temp;
}
}
// Function to compute the 2's complement of a binary number
void twosComplement(char *binary)
{
int len = strlen(binary);
int carry = 1; // Initialize carry to 1
for (int i = 0; i < len; i++)
{
if (binary[i] == '0')
{
binary[i] = '1';
}
else
{
binary[i] = '0';
}
```

```
// Add carry to the result
if (carry == 1)
{
if (binary[i] == '0')
{
binary[i] = '1';
carry = 0; // Carry is consumed
}
}
}
}
int main()
{
char binary[100];
printf("Enter a binary number: ");
scanf("%s", binary);
reverseBinaryString(binary); // Reverse the binary string
twosComplement(binary); // Compute the 2's complement
reverseBinaryString(binary); // Reverse the result back
printf("2's complement: %s\n", binary);
return 0;
}
```

- **Practical 25:** Write a C program to convert a Roman numeral to its decimal Equivalent.
- **Solution:**

```
#include <stdio.h>
#include <string.h>
// Function to convert a single Roman numeral character to its decimal
value
int romanCharToDecimal(char c)
{
switch (c)
```

```
{
case 'I':
return 1;
case 'V':
return 5;
case 'X':
return 10;
case 'L':
return 50;
case 'C':
return 100;
case 'D':
return 500;
case 'M':
return 1000;
default:
return 0;
}
}
// Function to convert a Roman numeral string to its decimal equivalent
int romanToDecimal(char *roman)
{
int decimal = 0;
int prevValue = 0;
// Iterate through the Roman numeral string from right to left
for (int i = strlen(roman) – 1; i >= 0; i–)
{
int currentValue = romanCharToDecimal(roman[i]);
// If the current value is smaller than the previous value, subtract it
if (currentValue < prevValue)
{
```

```
decimal –= currentValue;
}
else
{
decimal += currentValue;
}
prevValue = currentValue;
}
return decimal;
}
int main()
{
char romanNumeral[20];
printf("Enter a Roman numeral: ");
scanf("%s", romanNumeral);
int decimalEquivalent = romanToDecimal(romanNumeral);
printf("Decimal equivalent: %d\n", decimalEquivalent);
return 0;
}
```

- **Practical 26:** Write a c program on Given an unsorted array arr[] of size N. Rotate the array to the left (counter-clockwise direction) by D steps, where D is a positive integer.
- **Solution:**

```
#include <stdio.h>
// Function to reverse an array
void reverse(int arr[], int start, int end)
{
while (start < end)
{
int temp = arr[start];
arr[start] = arr[end];
arr[end] = temp;
```

```
start++;
end--;
}
}
// Function to rotate an array to the left by 'd' positions
void rotateLeft(int arr[], int N, int D)
{
D = D % N; // Ensure D is within array length
// Reverse the first D elements
reverse(arr, 0, D – 1);
// Reverse the remaining elements
reverse(arr, D, N – 1);
// Reverse the entire array
reverse(arr, 0, N – 1);
}
int main()
{
int N, D;
printf("Enter the size of the array: ");
scanf("%d", &N);
int arr[N];
printf("Enter the elements of the array: ");
for (int i = 0; i < N; i++)
{
scanf("%d", &arr[i]);
}
printf("Enter the number of positions to rotate left: ");
scanf("%d", &D);
rotateLeft(arr, N, D);
printf("Rotated array: ");
for (int i = 0; i < N; i++)
```

```
{
printf("%d ", arr[i]);
}
return 0;
}
```

- **Practical 27:** Write a c Program on given two sorted arrays arr1 and arr2 of size N and M respectively and an element K. The task is to find the element that would be at the kth position of the final sorted array. Explanation: Input: Array 1 – 1 4 2 3 5 Array 2 – 7 8 6 k = 5 Output: 5
- **Solution:**

```
#include <stdio.h>
// Function to find the k-th element in the merged array
int findKthElement(int arr1[], int N, int arr2[], int M, int k)
{
int i = 0, j = 0, count = 0, result;
while (i < N && j < M)
{
if (arr1[i] < arr2[j])
{
result = arr1[i];
i++;
}
else
{
result = arr2[j];
j++;
}
count++;
if (count == k)
{
return result;
```

```
}
}
// If we haven't reached k yet, continue from the remaining array
while (i < N)
{
result = arr1[i];
i++;
count++;
if (count == k)
{
return result;
}
}
while (j < M)
{
result = arr2[j];
j++;
count++;
if (count == k)
{
return result;
}
}
return –1; // Kth element not found
}
int main()
{
int N, M, k;
printf("Enter the size of the first array (N): ");
scanf("%d", &N);
int arr1[N];
```

```
printf("Enter the elements of the first array in sorted order: ");
for (int i = 0; i < N; i++)
{
scanf("%d", &arr1[i]);
}
printf("Enter the size of the second array (M): ");
scanf("%d", &M);
int arr2[M];
printf("Enter the elements of the second array in sorted order: ");
for (int i = 0; i < M; i++)
{
scanf("%d", &arr2[i]);
}
printf("Enter the value of k: ");
scanf("%d", &k);
int kthElement = findKthElement(arr1, N, arr2, M, k);
if (kthElement ! = –1)
{
printf("The k-th element in the merged array is: %d\n", kthElement);
}
else
{
printf("Invalid input. The k-th element is out of bounds.\n");
}
return 0;
}
```

- **Practical 28:** Write a c program to take multiline string input and print individual string length.
- Solution:

```
#include <stdio.h>
#include <string.h>
int main()
```

```
{
char input[1000]; // Assuming the maximum input size is 1000 characters
printf("Enter a multiline string (Ctrl+D or Ctrl+Z to end input):\n");
// Read multiline input until EOF (Ctrl+D or Ctrl+Z)
while (fgets(input, sizeof(input), stdin) != NULL)
{
// Remove the trailing newline character, if present
int len = strlen(input);
if (input[len – 1] == '\n')
{
input[len – 1] = '\0';
}
// Print the length of the current string
printf("Length: %d\n", strlen(input));
}
return 0;
}
```

- **Practical 29:** Write a c program to reverse the individual word of a given string Explanation:input: Welcome To Bytexl output: emocleW oT lxetyB.
- **Solution:**

```
#include <stdio.h>
#include <string.h>
// Function to reverse a word in the given string
void reverseWord(char *word, int start, int end)
{
while (start < end)
{
char temp = word[start];
word[start] = word[end];
word[end] = temp;
start++;
```

```
end--;
}
}
// Function to reverse individual words in a string
void reverseWordsInString(char *str)
{
int length = strlen(str);
int start = 0;
for (int end = 0; end <= length; end++)
{
if (str[end] == ' ' || str[end] == '\0')
{
reverseWord(str, start, end – 1);
start = end + 1;
}
}
}
int main()
{
char input[1000];
printf("Enter a string: ");
gets(input);
reverseWordsInString(input);
printf("Reversed string: %s\n", input);
return 0;
}
```

- **Practical 30:** Write a C program to enter a number and print it in words.
- **Solution:**

```
#include <stdio.h>
// Function to print a number in words for the ones place
void printOnes(int num)
```

```
{
switch (num)
{
case 1:
printf("One");
break;
case 2:
printf("Two");
break;
case 3:
printf("Three");
break;
case 4:
printf("Four");
break;
case 5:
printf("Five");
break;
case 6:
printf("Six");
break;
case 7:
printf("Seven");
break;
case 8:
printf("Eight");
break;
case 9:
printf("Nine");
break;
}
```

```
}
// Function to print a number in words for numbers between 10 and 19
void printTens(int num)
{
switch (num)
{
case 10:
printf("Ten");
break;
case 11:
printf("Eleven");
break;
case 12:
printf("Twelve");
break;
case 13:
printf("Thirteen");
break;
case 14:
printf("Fourteen");
break;
case 15:
printf("Fifteen");
break;
case 16:
printf("Sixteen");
break;
case 17:
printf("Seventeen");
break;
case 18:
```

```
printf("Eighteen");
break;
case 19:
printf("Nineteen");
break;
}
}
// Function to print a number in words for the tens place
void printTensPlace(int num)
{
switch (num)
{
case 2:
printf("Twenty");
break;
case 3:
printf("Thirty");
break;
case 4:
printf("Forty");
break;
case 5:
printf("Fifty");
break;
case 6:
printf("Sixty");
break;
case 7:
printf("Seventy");
break;
case 8:
```

```
printf("Eighty");
break;
case 9:
printf("Ninety");
break;
}
}
// Function to print a number in words
void printNumberInWords(int num)
{
if (num >= 1000 && num <= 9999)
{
int thousands = num / 1000;
printOnes(thousands);
printf(" Thousand ");
num %= 1000;
}
if (num >= 100)
{
int hundreds = num / 100;
printOnes(hundreds);
printf(" Hundred ");
num %= 100;
}
if (num >= 10 && num <= 19)
{
printTens(num);
}
else if (num >= 20)
{
int tens = num / 10;
```

```
printTensPlace(tens);
num %= 10;
if (num > 0)
{
printf("-");
}
}
if (num > 0)
{
printOnes(num);
}
printf("\n");
}
int main()
{
int num;
printf("Enter a number (up to 9999): ");
scanf("%d", &num);
if (num >= 0 && num <= 9999)
{
printNumberInWords(num);
}
else
{
printf("Number out of range.\n");
}
return 0;
}
```

- **Practical 31:** Write a for declaration & initialization of pointer.
- **Solution:**

```
#include<stdio.h>
```

```
void main()
{
int a=10, *p; // assign memory address of a to pointer variable p
p = &a;
printf("%d %d %d", a, *p, p);
}
```

- **Practical 32:** Write a program to print variable, address of pointer variable and pointer to pointer variable.
- **Solution:**

```
#include <stdio.h>
int main ()
{
int var;
int *ptr;
int **pptr;
var = 3000;
ptr = &var; // address of var
pptr = &ptr; // address of ptr using address of operator &
printf("Value of var = %d\n", var);
printf("Value available at *ptr = %d\n", *ptr);
printf("Value available at **pptr = %d\n", **pptr);
return 0;
}
```

- **Practical 33:** Write a program to swap value of two variables using pointer / call by reference.
- **Solution:**

```
#include<stdio.h>
int main()
{
int num1,num2;
printf("Enter value of num1 and num2: ");
scanf("%d %d",&num1, &num2);
```

```
//displaying numbers before swapping
printf("Before Swapping: num1 is: %d, num2 is: %d\n",num1,num2);
//calling the user defined function swap()
swap(&num1,&num2);
//displaying numbers after swapping
printf("After Swapping: num1 is: %d, num2 is: %d\n",num1,num2);
return 0;
}
```

- **Practical 34**: Write program for Call by Value.
- **Solution:**

```
#include<stdio.h>
void fun(int,int);
int main()
{
int A=10,B=20;
printf("\nValues before calling %d, %d",A,B);
fun(A,B);
printf("\nValues after calling %d, %d",A,B);
return 0;
}
void fun(int X,int Y)
{
X=11;
Y=22;
}
```

- **Practical 35:** Write a program for Call by Reference / Address.
- **Solution:**

```
#include<stdio.h>
void fun(int*,int*);
int main()
{
```

```
int A=10,B=20;
printf("\nValues before calling %d, %d",A,B);
fun(&A,&B);
printf("\nValues after calling %d, %d",A,B);
return 0;
}
void fun(int *X,int *Y)
{
*X=11;
*Y=22;
}
```

- **Practical 36:** Write a program to sum of two numbers using pointer to function.
- **Solution:**

```
#include<stdio.h>
int Sum(int,int);
int (*ptr)(int,int);
int main()
{
int a,b,rt;
printf("\nEnter 1st number: ");
scanf("%d",&a);
printf("\nEnter 2nd number: ");
scanf("%d",&b);
ptr = Sum;
rt = (*ptr)(a,b);
printf("\nThe sum is: %d",rt);
return 0;
}
int Sum(int x,int y)
{
return x + y;
```

```
}
```

- **Practical 36:** Write a C program to print the address of variable using pointer.
- **Solution:**

```
#include <stdio.h>
int main()
{
int number = 42; // Declare and initialize an integer variable
int *ptr; // Declare a pointer to an integer
ptr = &number; // Assign the address of 'number' to the pointer 'ptr'
printf("Address of 'number' variable: %p\n", &number);
printf("Address of 'number' using pointer 'ptr': %p\n", ptr);
return 0;
}
```

- **Practical 37:** Write a C a program for sorting using pointer.
- **Solution:**

```
#include <stdio.h>
void bubbleSort(int *arr, int size)
{
int temp;
for (int i = 0; i < size – 1; i++)
{
for (int j = 0; j < size – i – 1; j++)
{
if (*(arr + j) > *(arr + j + 1))
{
// Swap the elements using pointers
temp = *(arr + j);
*(arr + j) = *(arr + j + 1);
*(arr + j + 1) = temp;
```

```
}
}
}
}
int main()
{
int arr[] = {64, 34, 25, 12, 22, 11, 90};
int size = sizeof(arr) / sizeof(arr[0]);
printf("Original array: ");
for (int i = 0; i < size; i++)
{
printf("%d", arr[i]);
}
printf("\n");
bubbleSort(arr, size);
printf("Sorted array: ");
for (int i = 0; i < size; i++)
{
printf("%d ", arr[i]);
}
printf("\n");
return 0;
}
```

- **Practical 38:** Write a C a program to print value and address of a variable.
- **Solution:**

```
#include <stdio.h>
int main()
{
int number = 42; // Declare and initialize an integer variable
printf("Value of 'number' variable: %d\n", number);
printf("Address of 'number' variable: %p\n", &number);
```

```
return 0;
}
```

- **Practical 39:** Write a C a program to calculate sum of elements of an array using pointer.
- **Solution:**

```
#include <stdio.h>
int main()
{
int arr[] = {10, 20, 30, 40, 50};
int size = sizeof(arr) / sizeof(arr[0]);
int *ptr = arr; // Pointer pointing to the first element of the array
int sum = 0;
// Calculate the sum of elements using a pointer
for (int i = 0; i < size; i++)
{
sum += *ptr; // Add the value pointed to by 'ptr' to the sum
ptr++; // Move the pointer to the next element
}
printf("The sum of elements in the array is: %d\n", sum);
return 0;
}
```

- **Practical 40:** Write a C a program to print the address of character and the character of string using pointer.
- **Solution:**

```
#include <stdio.h>
int main()
{
char str[] = "Hello, World!";
char *ptr = str; // Pointer pointing to the first character of the string
printf("Address and characters of the string:\n");
// Loop through the string using the pointer
while (*ptr != '\0')
```

```
{
printf("Address: %p, Character: %c\n", ptr, *ptr);
ptr++; // Move the pointer to the next character
}
return 0;
}
```

INDEX